Ausgewählte Beiträge zur Anwenderkonferenz für Softwarequalität Test und Innovation 2013

ASQT 2013

Selected Topics to the User Conference on Software Quality, Test and Innovation 2013

books@ocg.at
Band 303

Conference Chairs:

Bernhard Peischl, Softnet Austria
Dietmar Wuksch, Cicero-Consulting GmbH

Program Committee:

Alexander van Ewijk, Sogeti Deutschland
Andreas Holzinger, Medizinische Universität Graz
Bernhard Peischl, Softnet Austria
Chrisitan Kop, Institut für Angewandte Informatik, Alpen-Adria Universität Klagenfurt
Dietmar Wuksch, Cicero Consulting
Franz Wotawa, Institut für Softwaretechnologie, Technische Universität Graz
Harry Sneed, Anecon Österreich
Horst Walther, HanseCom
Michael Heiss, Siemens Österreich
Peter Kieseberg, Secure Business Austria
Rudolf Ramler, Software Competence Center Hagenberg
Ruth Breu, Institut für Informatik, Universität Innsbruck
Siegfried Vössner, Institut für Maschinenbau- und Betriebsinformatik, Technische Universität Graz
Stefan Mohacsi, ATOS IT Solutions and Services
Wolfgang Herzner, Austrian Institute of Technology

Organization Committee:

Bernhard Peischl, Softnet Austria
Birgit Hofer, Institut für Softwaretechnologie, Technische Universität Graz
Dietmar Wuksch, Cicero Consulting
Petra Pichler, Technische Universität Graz & Softnet Austria
Sandra Lang, Softnet Austria

Sponsors:

Austrian Testing Board (ATB), Alser Straße 4, 1090 Wien, Österreich
Borland / Micro Focus, Fraunhoferstraße 7, 85737 Ismaning, Deutschland
Codenomicon GmbH, Clemensstrasse 30, 80803 München, Deutschland
Ranorex GmbH, Strassganger Straße, 289, 8053 Graz, Österreich

Dietmar Wuksch, Bernhard Peischl, Christian Kop (eds.)

Selected Topics to the User Conference on Software Quality, Test and Innovation 2013

ASQT 2013

September 19th – 20th, 2013
Graz, Austria

Scientific Editing Committee:

Druck: Druckerei Riegelnik
1080 Wien, Piaristengasse 19

ISBN: 978-3-85403-303-5

TABLE OF CONTENTS

PREFACE

On the 19th and 20th of September 2013, *Softnet Austria, Cicero Consulting* and the *Graz University of Technology* conducted the *11th User Conference on Software Quality, Test and Innovation (Anwenderkonferenz für Softwarequalität, Test und Innovation – ASQT 2013*). Over 90 *participants from industry and academia* attended the conference and contributed to vital discussions regarding the state of the practice and the scientific state of the art when it comes to corporate software quality. The *keynotes* focused on methods that allow engineers to *construct and operate reliable and trustworthy software systems* and in particular addressed the following contemporary topics:

- "Cost-Effective Model-Based Testing and Verification" (Univ.-Prof. Lionel C. Briand, Interdisciplinary Center for Security, Reliability and Trust, University of Luxembourg),
- "Establishing a Software Test Center as a Service" (Robert Korošec, AVL List GmbH, Graz, Austria)
- "The Impact of Tools to Software Quality" (Oskar Slotosch, Validas AG, Munich, Germany)
- "Model-based Security Testing and its Application to Industrial Case Studies: Security Risk Analysis and Smart Fuzzing in Practice" (Axel Rennoch, Fraunhofer FOKUS, Berlin, Germany)

The *inaugural address* specifically discussed Austria's role as a location for industry and high-tech companies ("Industrie- und Hightechstandort Österreich? Erfahrungen, Analysen, Empfehlungen", Hellmut Longin, CEO/Chairman of RHI AG). Gert Polli - long-standing head of Austira's Federal Office for the Protection of the Constitution (BTV, Bundesamt für Verfassungsschutz und Terrorismusbekämpfung) – provided insights on economic espionage and on how intelligence services exploit, for example, flight schedules and related data, credit and debit card transactions and movements on accounts. In his *closing speech* "Die Affäre Snowden – Ein längst fälliger Wake-Up Call für die Europäer" he pointed out the need to *scrutinize data exchange between the USA and Europe,* and numerous issues around data protection, security and European Cloud providers.
Besides of these invited contributions, numerous regular talks and presentations in two tracks (one track on innovation and quality, another track on software testing) addressed pain-points and prevailing topics in software quality assurance. Several contributions focused on the *target topic* of ASQT 2013 – information security – in terms of showing best practices for engineering trustworthy and secure software systems. Among them, tool-based finding of security leaks, the role of static analysis techniques in detecting security leaks and the controversial question whether information security is rather a business topic than just an IT topic. *Researchers* and *practitioners* further discussed *evidence-based methods* for engineering *secure and trustworthy software* in terms of security testing techniques like penetration testing via combinational designs and security testing with attack patterns.
Finally our gratitude goes to all participants, the more than 35 lecturers and our sponsors (Ranorex GmbH, Borland Software Corporation, Codenomicon GmbH, and the Austrian Testing Board) for making ASQT 2013 in Graz a vital and memorable event.

Graz, March 2014

Dietmar Wuksch, Bernhard Peischl and Christian Kop

KEYNOTES

COST-EFFECTIVE MODEL-BASED TESTING AND VERIFICATION

Lionel C. Briand
Software Verification and Validation Laboratory
Interdisciplinary Centre for ICT Security, Reliability, and Trust (SnT),
University of Luxembourg,
SnT Centre
4, rue Alphonse Weicker
L-2721 Luxembourg, Luxembourg

Cost-effective testing must be automated. Automation must not only include test execution and logging, but also test case generation, including automated verdicts (or oracles). This is especially important in the context of systems with long lifespans, having to adapt to frequent requirements changes. This presentation will report on 20 years of experience and innovation in the area of model-based testing and verification. Current technology still has a long way to go, thus warranting the need for applied research. But the benefits of model-based testing can already be significant if the right technology is tailored to the application domain, objectives, and specific system architecture, and carefully evaluated.

ESTABLISHING A SOFTWARE TEST CENTER AS SERVICE

Robert Korošec
AVL List GmbH
Hans-List-Platz 1
8020 Graz, Austria

In the automotive industry, AVL is the world's largest private and independent company for the engineering and production of instrumentation and test systems. This presentation describes lessons learned during establishing and operating a central "Software Test Center" as service for product development segments, internal as well as external customers. The organizational development of a Test Center as service needs to deal with business as well as SW engineering considerations and some extra challenges in a globally distributed SW development group releasing products for global customers. The cooperation with research institutions helps to industrialize new test methodology approaches; some examples of research activities will be covered.

Currently the SW group is moving from a classical iterative to a lean and agile approach. Main goals are to increase first time quality and to reduce time to market for innovative SW solutions. What is well understood and documented on a team level, still offers challenges for a large and globally distributed organization. First experiences on the task to scale agility are presented.

MODEL-BASED SECURITY TESTING AND ITS APPLICATIONS TO INDUSTRIAL CASE STUDIES: SECURITY RISK ANALYSIS AND SMART FUZZING IN PRACTICE

Axel Rennoch
Fraunhofer Institute for Open Communication Systems FOKUS
Kaiserin-Augusta-Allee 31,
10589 Berlin, Germany

Model-based Security Testing (MBST) is a relatively new field and especially focuses on a systematic and efficient specification, generation, or documentation of test objectives, security test cases, and security test suites. In particular, the combination of security modeling and test generation approaches is still a challenge in research and of high interest for industrial applications. The ITEA project DIAMONDS develops efficient and automated MBST methods for highly secure systems in multiple industrial domains (e.g. banking, automotive, telecommunication, industrial automation etc.). Amongst others, the project has a special focus on advanced model-based security testing methods that combine different security testing techniques to obtain improved results. Model-based fuzz testing allows for the automated and semi-automated detection of vulnerabilities related to missing input validation and the detection of flaws in dedicated security controls.

THE IMPACT OF TOOLS TO SOFTWARE QUALITY

Oscar Slotosch
Validas AG
Arnulfstraße 27
80335 München, Germany

The quality of a software product does not only depend on the product development process starting from requirements and including tests, but also on the used tools. There are many tool errors that have caused severe product failures. Therefore many safety standards require to analyze the potential impact of tools to the product. This analysis depends on the usage of the tools. Tools are classified according to the impact on their potential failures can have to the product. Tools that might insert or oversee product errors are classified as having "Confidence Need". In the talk an overview of the safety standards is given and it is shown how the required tool confidence can be created by systematically testing the tool in order to show the absence of the critical errors. We present a model that helps to determine the critical tool errors and is used as a basis for development of qualification kits that provide the required confidence. As an outlook a brief sketch of the Eclipse roadmap towards tool qualification is given.

REGULAR PAPERS

TOOL-BASED FINDING OF SECURITY LEAKS IN LARGE SOFTWARE PROJECTS

Christof Dallermassl
Unycom GmbH
St.-Peter-Gürtel 10
8042 Graz, Austria
christof.dallermassl@unycom.com

Abstract
Due to the large amount of source code, finding and closing security leaks in large web applications – especially with regard to Cross-Site Scripting (XSS) and SQL Injection – is as challenging as the planning of a corresponding code cleanup. Automated tools that combine the advantages of static source code analysis and dynamic run time analysis can help to make this process considerably faster, simpler, and easier to plan.

1. Background

Unycom develops software for the management of intellectual property. This software is mainly used by large enterprises that handle thousands of property files, starting with the disclosure of an invention by the inventors themselves until the expiry of the granted patent. It helps to administrate the entered data, but also supports the communication with external partners, patent offices, and other involved parties.

The Web-based application was originally based on a self-developed Java framework. It used Java Server Pages (JSP) as presentation layer, Java objects in the business layer and Oracle as the relational database backend. Later, a new and state-of-the-art technology stack was added that introduced Google Web Toolkit (GWT) on the client side, UML as data model, and the Spring and Hibernate frameworks for the object-relational mapping to the Oracle database system on the server side. All in all, the source code is quite heterogeneous and consists of around 8000 Java classes and 4000 SQL files, each having close to 1 million lines of code, and additionally more than 1000 JSP pages.

2. The Problem

The Open Web Application Security Project (OWASP) [3] rates Cross-Site Scripting (XSS) and SQL Injection as extremely dangerous – both for the users of the system (XSS) and for the data integrity of the system itself (SQL Injection). Though it is comparatively easy to fix these security leaks, it is often difficult to find all affected lines of source code.

Another problem that is less of a technical than of an organizational nature is the planning of such security measures. As the amount of security leaks to be found is completely unknown at the beginning of the process, the amount of time and manpower needed for their elimination is hard to estimate.

3. The Solution

The solution approach chosen by Unycom tried to approach both the technical and the organizational side. It used two different technologies to improve the detection of security leaks: the source code was statically analyzed with the help of a commercial tool, but for various different reasons, this task proved to be very difficult and time-consuming:

- The large number of classes with a high degree of abstraction (such as interfaces with more than hundred possible implementations) resulted in a very large static execution tree which in turn resulted in very long scan times and timeouts during the analysis phase.
- The execution path of the system is partly configured in the database and therefore not visible to any tool by just analyzing the Java source code.
- Third party libraries that are only delivered as binaries are seen as black boxes and any insecure data handling inside these black boxes were invisible in the static code analysis.

This is where the second technology was applied: a tool developed in-house that was used to analyze the dynamic data flow during the execution of the application. This so-called *Dynamic Taint Propagation* [1,2] method dynamically traces all data from predefined sources to predefined sinks. The tool is able to dynamically follow potentially dangerous data from the user interface or values read from the database (*sources*) to database queries or HTML creation (*sinks*) during runtime. If the data values do not pass some defined *sanitizer* code between a data source and a sink, a potential SQL injection or XSS attack is reported.

The results gained from the dynamic analysis allowed the definition of new static scan rules for better and optimized source, sink, and sanitizer code detection. Once the rules were optimized, the developers were able to efficiently fix the detected security leaks. Incremental scans gave a good overview of the progress made and were used as a forecast for the total duration until all leaks were found and fixed.

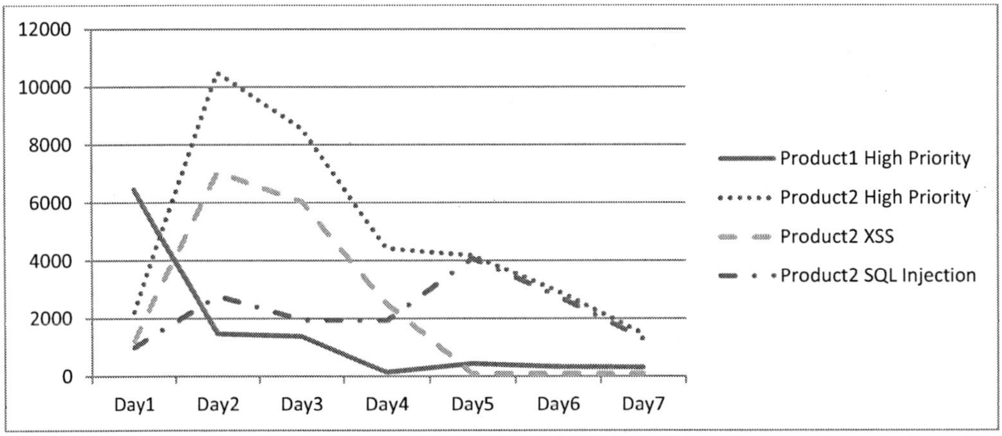

Figure 1: The number of security leaks detected by the static source code analysis tool.

Figure 1 shows the absolute number of leaks detected in the scan in two different applications as well as separate numbers for XSS and SQL Injection. The increasing number at the beginning was the result of the optimization process of the scan rules. The decreasing numbers show the progress of fixing the leaks.

4. Results

Both the static and the dynamic runtime analyses gave good results. However, using the output of the taint propagation tool to refine the scan rules of the static source code analysis tool significantly increased the number, but also the quality of found problems.

In conclusion, it can be said that both tools help to save an enormous amount of time in comparison to the manual search for security leaks. They provide a quick indicator for the quality of source code and are therefore powerful tools for the fixing of security leaks and its planning. Additionally, the use of incremental scans ensures good progress documentation.

REFERENCES

[1] Chess, B., West, J., Dynamic Taint Propagation, Blackhat Conference 2008

[2] Haldar, V., Chandra, D., Franz, M., Dynamic Taint Propagation for Java, ACSAC 2005

[3] OWASP, The Open Web Application Security Project, http://www.owasp.com

THE ROLE OF AUTOMATED STATIC ANALYSIS IN DETECTING SECURITY LEAKS

Harry Sneed and Thomas Bucsics
ANECON Software Design u. Beratung GmbH,
Alser Straße 4 / Hof 1
1090 Vienna, Austria
{harry.sneed, thomas.bucsics}@anecon.com

1. Purpose of Static Analysis

Static analysis is one of many approaches aimed at detecting faults in software. It is a process of evaluating a system or component based on its form, structure, content or documentation which does not require program execution [1]. Code inspections are one example of a classic static analysis technique relying on manual examination of the code to detect errors, violations of coding conventions and other potential problems. Another type of static analysis is the use of automated tools to identify anomalies in the code such as non-compliance with coding standards, uncaught runtime exceptions, redundant code, incorrect use of variables, division by zero and potential memory leaks. This is referred to as automated static analysis [2].

2. Detecting Code Deficiencies

There are now many tools available to support automated static analysis – tools like Software Sonar, Conformity and SoftAudit. In selecting a proper tool, the main question is what types of deficiencies are reported by the tool [4]. Another question has to do with the number of false positives the tool produces that is how many defects or deficiencies are by closer examination not really true. When tools produce a great number of false positives, this only distracts from locating the real problems. As to the types of true problems reported, it is important to have a problem classification schema. From the viewpoint of software quality there are five major classes of code problems:

- missing code = statements that should be there and is not
- redundant code = statements that are there and should not be
- erroneous code = statements that may cause an error when the code is executed
- non-conform code = statements which violate a local standard or coding convention
- deficient code = statements that reduce the overall quality of the code, maintainability, portability, testability, etc.

3. Case Study in Detecting Code Deficiencies

A study performed at the North Carolina State University on over 3 million lines of C++ Code from the Nortel Networks Corporation demonstrate how effective automated static analysis can be [8]. Using the tool "Flexlint" the researcher were able to detect more than 136.000 problems or one problem for every 22 code statements. Even though this code had been in operation for over three years there remained a significant technical debt. The problems uncovered by the automated static analysis also correlated well to the defects discovered during the prerelease testing with an accuracy of 83%. That implies that 83% of the erroneous modules could have been identified already through static analysis.
The authors of the study classified the defects they found into four levels of severity in reference to the IEEE fault classification schema, critical defects, major defects, minor defects and coding standard violations. Of the defects uncovered in the static analysis, 20% were critical, 39% were major and 41% were minor. Coding standard violations were not included in this count. Based on their findings, the authors came to the conclusion that automated static analysis can be considered an effective and economic means of detecting problematic code modules [5].

4. Security Threats to Java Code

Next to reliability, efficiency, usability, portability and maintainability, security has become one of the main non-functional concerns in developing new IT systems. Developers should pay attention to the many security rules they should follow when writing code, rules such as validating inputs, minimizing accessibility to classes and member, and avoiding public static nonfunctional fields. Such rules are intended to reduce the likelihood of security vulnerabilities in the code. Most if not all of these rules can be controlled via static analysis [3].
One of the most frequent security rule violations is that of determining accessibility. From a security perspective developers should minimize accessibility, i.e. public access should be restricted to the absolute minimum. For instance, if a class member is part of neither a published API nor an implemented package, it should be declared private. This defends it against attacks from outside and unintended use within the package. Variables should never be declared public and methods only when they are members of a public interface. Methods may be declared protected if they are to be accessed by other classes within the same package. Unfortunately the compiler may widen the accessibility of a class member if the class in which it is contained is nested within another class. Therefore, nested classes should also be prohibited. There is no threat of trusted classes unintentionally accessing the widened package-private members. However, package-private members can come under attack if hostile code infiltrates the package. A package attack occurs when new classes are added or old classes are replaced in an existing package. Such an attack is possible when trusted code is hosted on a virtual machine alongside untrusted code. The key to preventing such package attacks in insecure environments is to properly isolate code using the access protection mechanism [7].
Another source of security threat are corrupted inputs. All input objects need to be validated before they are used. However, it is not enough to validate them. If the input object is mutable, it is equally important to make a copy of that object before validating it. Otherwise, the sender of the input object can mutate it to exploit race conditions in the receiving method. A typical exploitable race condition is a "time-of-check", "time of use" inconsistency, where a mutable input has one state when it is checked and another state when it is used. To ensure against such undesired mutation, it is necessary to copy incoming objects. The simplest way of creating a copy of a mutable object is via the cloning mechanism. If the object is clonable and has a public clone method, the callers can call that method

to create a copy of the object. It may still be necessary to create a manual copy of the mutable object. This is done by retrieving the state of the original object and creating a new instance of that state. In any case the receiver of input object must protect himself against malicious mutation of those objects. A third cause of security intrusion is the unauthorized construction of security-sensitive classes. That can occur in two ways: when a class is clonable and when a class is serializable. In the case of cloning, a caller can acquire an instance of a cloneable class by invoking the public clone method. In the case of deserialization, an instance of a serializable class can be reconstructed from a serialized stream. In both cases the intruder is producing instances of a class without invoking a constructor of that class. This type of unauthorized construction can be prevented by declaring the classes as final. All of these security threats can be avoided by defensive coding techniques. Developers have the possibility of using protective features such as access restriction, object duplication and finalizing declaration. However, their adherence to these techniques needs to be verified.

5. Detecting Security Defects in Java Code

Most of the security threats in the code can be detected through automated static analysis. JavAudit is representative of tools which perform such an analysis. It enforces 12 rules for secure Java code. These rules are:

1) Guard against the allocation of uninitialized objects
2) Limit access to classes and their members
3) Declare all classes and methods as final
4) Prevent new classes from being added to finished packages
5) Forbid the nesting of classes
6) Avoid the signing of code
7) Put all of the code in one jar or archive file
8) Define the classes as uncloneable
9) Make the classes unserializeable
10) Make the classes undeserializeable
11) Forbid company classes by name
12) Avoid the hardwiring of sensitive data in the code

JavAudit scans the code for infringement of these rules. All of the rule violations can be recognized except for the last one. Here it is not possible to distinguish between sensitive and non-sensitive data. Therefore it is better not to use hard-wired text in the code at all. If it is, then it can be easily recognized and reported [6].

6. Conclusion

Experience with *SofAudit* and similar source analysis tools shows that it is definitely worthwhile to invest in statically analyzing source code before starting to test it. Most of the potential security leaks are to be found in the code. Testing only confirms that they are there. The best and cheapest way to eliminate them is by uncovering them in the code before the code is executed. In this respect static analysis is definitely preferable to dynamic testing.

REFERENCES

[1] Ayewah, N., Pugh, W., "Using Static Analysis to find Bugs", IEEE Software Magazine, Sept. 208, p. 22

[2] Chess, B.: "Improving Computer Security using extended Static Checking", Proc. of IEEE Symposium on Security and Privacy, 2002, p. 160

[3] Lai, C., "Java Insecurity – accounting for Subtleties that can compromise Code", IEEE Software Magazine, Jan. 2008, p. 13

[4] Nagappan, N., Ball, T., "Static Analysis Tools as early Indicators of Prerelease Defect Density", IEEE Proc. of Int.Conf. on S.E. (ICSE2005), p. 580

[5] Nakajo, T., "A Case History Analysis of Software Error Cause and Effect Relationships", IEEE Trans. on S.E., Vol. 17, Nr. 8, August, 1991, S. 830

[6] Sneed, H. "SoftAudit – A Tool for checking and measuring source Code", ANECON Report, Wien, 2011

[7] Viega, J., McGRAW, G., FELTEN, E.: "Statically Scanning Java Code – Finding Security Vulnerabilities", IEEE Software Magazine, Sept. 2000, p. 68

[8] Zheng, J.,Williams, L.,Nagappan, N., Snipes, W.: "On the Value of Static Analysis for Fault Detection in Software", IEEE Trans. on S.E., Vol. 32, No. 4, April 2006, p. 240

Information Security is a Business Issue . . . ! Or isn't it? And what about Privacy?

Roel Kragten
Cicero Consulting
Paracelsusgasse 14
9020 Klagenfurt, Paracelsusgasse 14
roel.kragten@cicero-consulting.com

Summary
The past five to ten years have shown clear trends where IT-security moves in the direction of information security. Therefore, the responsibility is moving away from the technical, towards the business disciplines. This parallels the development of the role of IT in an organization. IT is becoming a business factor more and more and so is information security. In addition, actually, so is privacy security.

1. Introduction

In Deloitte's Business Balance Survey 2009, over 38% of 1868 Enterprises in 28 EMEA-countries, the Americas and the Asia-Pacific-Area responded not being aware of any security incidents in the company. Another 13% was aware of the kinds of possible incidents (as opposed to the first 38%) but was not able to say if any occurrences had taken place in their own enterprise. An additional 14% was not willing to answer this question, although anonymously. In 2011, two years later, there were over 2000 participants in 37 countries. Still approx. 37% were unaware of any incidents and another 20% knew about the possibilities but did not know if any of these possible incidents might have happened in their enterprises.

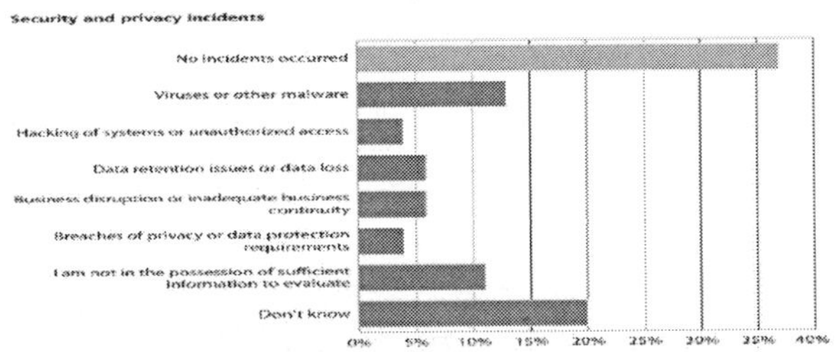

Figure 1: Deloitte Business Balance Survey, 2011

Wikileaks, Vatileaks and e.g. scandals in the press about health data of ÖBB (Austrian railways) - employees becoming public or recently leaking test results of Austria's PISA-participants make us understand the question of many managers: "This cannot happen to us, can it?"

Therefore, it is understandable that more and more often the business side in companies engages in these issues, especially since very often organizational causes can be found:

- Missing governance principles
- Access control
- Consequence at the workplace
- Missing business continuity measures (IT-supported, but in principle a business issue)
- ...

McKinsey published an article in August 2013 with 3 main conclusions:

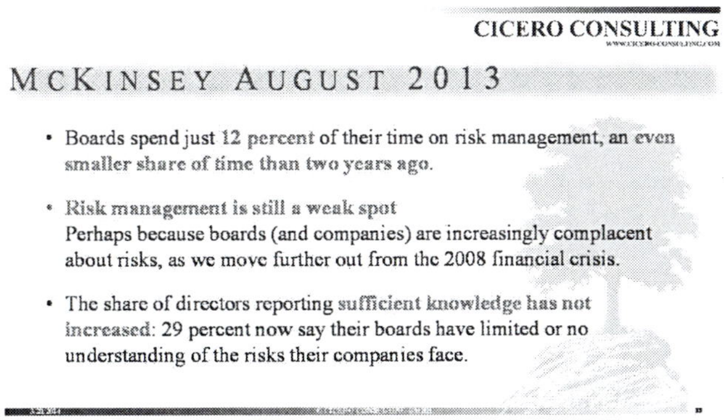

Figure 2: McKinsey 2013 confirms Deloitte 2011

Quality of IT, especially in the security and privacy areas is growingly a requirements issue. Therefore, we can recognize a few trends and issues.

2. The more important Security / Privacy, the more the CISO moves out of IT

In industries where the importance of integrity and the confidentiality of personal data are paramount (e.g. financial – and social services, health care and energy) C-Level managers like the risk officer, the security officer (when different) and the chief information officer are moving away from IT. Growing awareness of cyber security and the necessary protection of critical infrastructure are actually reinforcing this movement.

In organizations, that already have completed this transformation have a governance that functions more effectively. Especially since arguments for change and action are now coming from the, mostly more understandable, business area and the connected powers of decision are positioned there where the needs are.

3. A CISO and/or CIO outside IT improves Business-Engagement in Security

In the studies, mentioned above, 54% of the organizations had business managers that felt affected by security and privacy issues. But affected doesn't mean involved. When the C-Level responsible managers like CISO, CRO or CIO are operating outside the IT department 78% of the business management also feels involved. The company strategy of these enterprises mentions issues like information security and privacy. Therefore, measures are more easily defined, actually taken and implemented.

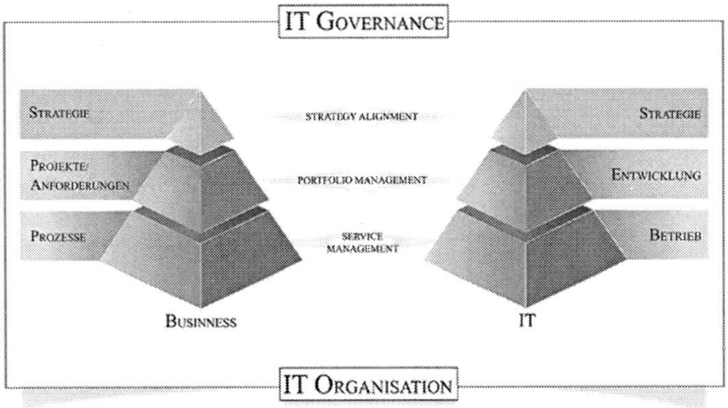

Figure 3: Business Involvement and IT-Governance

4. Actually too little Resources are available for Security and Privacy

Especially in smaller enterprises, it is very unusual if outside the IT a security - or risk – officer is installed. In these kinds of companies, mostly the director of the company would be responsible for taking up these issues. The awareness for this responsibility in these small companies is not high. Should a director feel responsible it is still difficult to implement measures, because the resources are not available. In larger enterprises, that have no C-Level responsibility for Information security or privacy installed on the business side, the issue is the same. Information security and privacy are seen as IT issues, IT cost have to be reduced – so, less resources for information security and privacy.

5. Privacy is just a Security add-on

Eighty percent of the enterprises without a CISO do not have Privacy-Management at all. And there are almost no enterprises that install Privacy-Management without information security. Actually, a total of 53% of all interviewed enterprises have no visible privacy measures at all. A difference between sectors is not recognizable.

6. Advise

Implement a good Governance and take the information security and privacy responsibility out of IT. Make these issues a part of the company strategy and follow the implementation of derived measures closely until satisfactory.

FROM FAULT LOCALIZATION OF PROGRAMS WRITTEN IN 3RD LEVEL LANGUAGES TO SPREADSHEETS

Birgit Hofer, Franz Wotawa
Graz University of Technology, Institute for Software Technology,
8010 Graz, Austria
{bhofer,wotawa}@ist.tugraz.at

Abstract

This paper aims to give insights into one of the current research topics in the field of automated debugging. In particular, this paper addresses the first step of the debugging process, i.e. fault localization, for the two distinct domains: (1) Software written in imperative or object-oriented languages and (2) Spreadsheets.

1. Software Debugging

Every year, the requirements on software increase. The trends in software engineering are towards increasing functionality, increasing flexibility and decreasing the time-to-market. However, these trends come with a price: Because of the high market competitiveness and the pressure to be the first on market, the testing and debugging stay behind. Many faults remain undetected in the pre-release phase because of superficial testing. Even worse, detected bugs are often not corrected because the next steps after error detection, i.e., fault localization and correction, are rarely automated. Therefore, not all of the discovered errors can be corrected in an acceptable amount of time. Often, programmers can only correct the most critical bugs. As a consequence, debugging has been identified as a bottleneck for improving reliability [1].

Traditionally, debugging was done manually by adding print statements to the source code. Print statements allow the programmer to check if certain statements are reached during the execution and to determine the value of a variable at a certain point in the program. Nowadays, debugging tools improve the manual debugging approach: Breakpoints and step-by-step execution allow the observation of program states. However, this step-by-step execution is very time consuming because a programmer has to manually narrow down the search space by introducing break points and comparing intermediate variable values of the program with the expected values. Moreover, setting the right break points or obtaining the right information from a program in order to speed up the debugging process, is a hard task. Even worse, in many cases a programmer does not fully understand a program and can hardly find such optimal decisions. Consequently, there is a strong need for tools guiding the programmer through the fault localization process. Such tools should point to source code locations where the fault is most likely to be found.

On the academic side, automated debugging techniques and prototypes are available which help to narrow down possible fault locations. However, these approaches are hardly used by programmers. The main reason for the refusal to use these techniques is that they are not mature. In addition, debugging tools do not smoothly integrate in the available IDEs. Furthermore, these debugging tools fail to identify unique root causes and still leave a lot of work for the programmer. Moreover, the techniques applied in debugging tools can also be computationally demanding, which prevents them from being used for large-scaled programs and in an interactive manner. There is a strong need for improving existing debugging techniques so that they are accepted by programmers.

At the Institute of Software Technology, we have developed several techniques that improve fault localization of programs written in imperative or object-oriented languages (i.e. 3rd generation languages). In particular, techniques in the field of model-based software debugging [5, 9, 10] have been developed in the last years. In addition, techniques combining existing fault localization techniques have been developed, e.g. [4].

2. Spreadsheet Debugging

Our work focuses not only on the fault localization in programs written in 3rd generation languages but also on the fault localization in other domains. Recently, we started to adapt existing fault localization techniques to the domain of end-user programs. In particular, we have developed tools for supporting the fault localization process in spreadsheets. Spreadsheets are by far the most prominent example of end-user programming. End-user programmers vastly outnumber professional ones. Panko and Port [8] state that spreadsheets are used in more than 95 % of the U.S. companies for a variety of purposes, e.g. for financial reporting, forecasting, planning, data management and chart creation. Furthermore, companies often use dozens or even hundreds of spreadsheet applications which often tend to be large and complex comprising hundreds or even thousands of formulas. Considering that important decisions are often based on spreadsheets, it is desirable that spreadsheets are free from errors. Unfortunately, numerous studies have shown that existing spreadsheets contain redundancy and errors at an alarmingly high rate [3]. Panko published the results of field audits for spreadsheets on a website (http://panko.shidler.hawaii.edu/ssr/): On average, 88 % of the spreadsheets investigated between 1995 and 2007 contained at least one error. However, when basing business decisions on spreadsheets, errors can lead to a significant financial loss or to other business risks – as reported on the web site of the European Spreadsheet Risk Interest Group (http://www.eusprig.org/horror-stories.htm).

We adapted debugging approaches for 3rd generation languages, e.g. model-based software debugging (MBSD) [9], spectrum-based fault localization (SFL) [2] and spectrum-enhanced dynamic slicing (SENDYS) [4], to the spreadsheet domain [6]. First empirical results show that MBSD, SFL and SENDYS are promising techniques for debugging spreadsheets. These techniques produce short lists of possibly faulty cells and thus they allow shorter debugging times. Unfortunately, the number of diagnoses (i.e. explanations of an observed misbehavior) can still be huge. When the user changes all cells that are contained in a diagnosis in the right way, the user could repair the spreadsheet. However, fault localization approaches cannot give the user hints how to change the cells.

We are confident that the information how cells should be changed is an important support for the user. Therefore, we propose a novel approach that automatically creates versions, i.e. mutants, of the spreadsheet that satisfy the given test case [7]. This approach uses concepts of Genetic Programming: Change and survival of the fittest. Change is realized by randomly mutating the cell's formulas. Allowed mutations are – amongst others – the change of Boolean values, the permutation of digits, the change of signs, the change of references and the change of operators. Similar to nature, only the fittest mutants will survive in Genetic Programming. The fittest mutants are determined by means of a fitness function. This function takes into consideration how many output cells in the mutant produce a correct result. Unless an improvement compared to the initial faulty spreadsheet could be detected, the mutant is thrown away. With this approach, many mutants could be generated that satisfy a given test case. In order to avoid that a user is overwhelmed by too many correction suggestions, we plan to offer a filtering mechanism: We automatically create distinguishing test cases [10] for the mutants. A test case is a distinguishing test case if there is at least one output cell where the computed values of two versions of a spreadsheet, i.e. two mutants, differ on the same input. A prototype called MuSSCO (short for Mutation Supported Spreadsheet Correction) allows to experiment with distinguishing test cases and is publicly available (http://mussco.ist.tugraz.at/). Future work in this field includes user studies to examine if MuSSCO can help end-users to faster find and correct faults in spreadsheets.

REFERENCES

[1] Abreu, R., Zoeteweij, P., and van Gemund, A. J. C., "An evaluation of similarity coefficients for software fault localization," in: Proceedings of the 12th Pacific Rim International Symposium on Dependable Computing, ser. PRDC '06. Washington, DC, USA: IEEE Computer Society, pp. 39–46, 2006.

[2] Abreu, R., Zoeteweij, R., Golsteijn, P., and van Gemund, A. J. C., "A practical evaluation of spectrum-based fault localization," Journal of Systems & Software (JSS), vol. 82, no. 11, pp. 1780–1792, 2009.

[3] Chadwick, D., Knight, B., and Rajalingham, K., "Quality control in spreadsheets: A visual approach using color codings to reduce errors in formulae," Software Quality Journal, vol. 9, no. 2, pp. 133–143, 2001.

[4] Hofer, B., and Wotawa, F. "Spectrum enhanced dynamic slicing for better fault localization." Proceedings of 20th European Conference on Artificial Intelligence (ECAI 2012), pp. 420–425. Doi: 10.3233/978-1-61499-098-7-420

[5] Hofer, B. and Wotawa, F., "Combining slicing and constraint solving for better debugging: The CONBAS approach," Advances in Software Engineering, vol. 2012, Article ID 628571, 18 pages, 2012. Doi: 10.1155/2012/628571

[6] Hofer, B., Riboira, A., Wotawa, F., Abreu, R., and Getzner, E., "On the empirical evaluation of fault localization techniques for spreadsheets." Proceedings of 16th International Conference on Fundamental Approaches to Software Engineering, FASE 2013, Held as Part of the European Joint Conferences on Theory and Practice of Software, ETAPS 2013, pp. 68–82, 2013. Doi: 10.1007/978-3-642-37057-1

[7] Hofer, B. and Wotawa, F., "Mutation-based spreadsheet debugging" 4th IEEE International Workshop on Program Debugging, 2013 IEEE International Symposium on Software Reliability Engineering Workshops (ISSREW), pp. 132-137, 2013. Doi: 10.1109/ISSREW.2013.6688892

[8] R. R. Panko and D. N. Port, "End user computing: The dark matter (and dark energy) of corporate IT," in HICSS. IEEE Computer Society, 2012, pp. 4603–4612.

[9] Wotawa, F. and Nica, M., "On the compilation of programs into their equivalent constraint representation," in: Informatica (Slovenia), vol. 32, no. 4, pp. 359–371, 2008.

[10] Wotawa, F., Nica, M. and Aichernig, B. K., "Generating distinguishing tests using the minion constraint solver," in: Third International Conference on Software Testing, Verification and Validation, ICST 2010, Workshops Proceedings, IEEE Computer Society, pp. 325-330, 2010. Doi: 10.1109/ICSTW.2010.11

A CUSTOM-CLASSIFICATION OF COMMUNICATION FLOW IN A CLIENT-SERVER MODEL

Aleksandar Hudic[a], Elise Revell[b] and Dimitris E. Simos[1a]

[a]SBA Research

Vienna, 1040, Austria

{ahudic,dsimos}@sba-research.org

[b]Kelisec AB

Stockholm, SE 101 23, Sweden

elise.revell@kelisec.com

In this work we describe a communication method, first proposed in [1] and extended in [2], which gives an approach for establishing secure communication between two entities. In addition, we present a security classification of its communication flow. The original concept given in [1] proposed a key generation method that produces symmetric keys in the nodes themselves without revealing them over an insecure channel. This method assumes a trusted third-party, i.e. a secure server (SeS) and clients (nodes) that want to become members of a secure network. Based on the communication method given in [2], we propose the following four phases of renewal, authentication, key generation and key scheduling for a client-server model. For the state-of-the-art of client-server models we refer to [3]. A high-level overview of these phases can be seen in Figure 1.

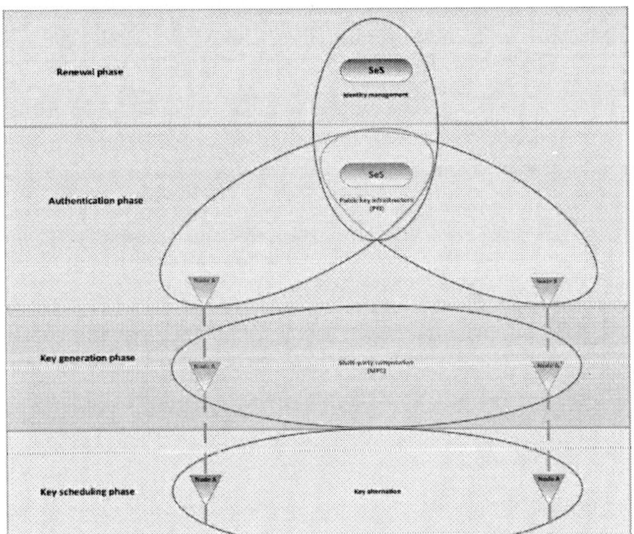

Figure 1. Proposed communication phases.

a) Renewal phase: In this initial phase of the communication method described in Figure 1. In this phase, there are nodes that are already registered in the secure network but not necessarily be

1 Authors are listed in alphabetical order.

authenticated (see also the following phase). Therefore, the authentication tokens of the nodes are renewed in order to avoid replay attacks.
b) Authentication phase: Is the second phase of the proposed communication method. We consider, for this phase as an example, the following scenario: *There is a node that wants to become a member of the Secure network. In practical terms, a node could be a bank client operating a transaction through a mobile phone or a tablet. The identity of this node is not known beforehand and therefore we can assume that it can also be a malicious attacker. Therefore, at this phase secure authentication of the node has to be ensured.*

Secure authentication in this phase is ensured through Public Key Infrastructure (PKI), whereby we assume that each entity in the communication process has been uniquely assigned public/private keys. PKI keys are used to perform and ensure secure mutual authentication process between the nodes and SeS server.

c) Key generation phase: The key generation phase encompass a key generation method for symmetric encryption without revealing the generated keys over an insecure channel. To avoid any kind of insecure key distribution over the secure network, the key generation process of this phase is conducted in such a manner that the keys are generated within the corresponding nodes.

d) Key scheduling phase: The last phase of the proposed communication method provides a key alternation process in order to enhance security. The symmetric key used for session is changing during one communication session, and potentially can increase the security of the communication method.

The baseline of each communication process, between two entities, is to ensure confidentiality, integrity and authenticity of the corresponding entities. Therefore, proper security mechanisms have to be embraced in order to protect the communication channel and the parties that are using it. The concept given in [2], gives an overview of a security architecture in order to provide secure communication between two entities (nodes).

The communication scheme of [1] and [2] can be defined as two independent processes:

- Node to node communication
- Node to server communication

Node to node communication - Two particular nodes are trying to directly establish a shared session and generate a symmetric key.
Node to server communication - Both of the nodes that are participating in the communication, have to be registered and authenticated in the secure network. In order this to be achieved they need to have a direct correspondence with the server.
We now aim to a classification of the communication flow in the client-server model we have used so far. Our goal is to accomplish this classification over the four phases described in Figure 1 by classifying their security levels.

We propose a general security classification, in respect to the communication scheme, by defining the following security classes:

- Low security
- Medium security

• High security

The four phases of the communication method are considered together with the security classes in order to investigate security aspects of the communication flow. We target on communication flow of corresponding parties that are involved in the works mentioned by [1] and [2], i.e. the nodes and the SeS server. The proposed security classes are used to define a rough security classification that represent an initial point of our future security analysis. Through these security classes we would like to investigate and analyze security concerns related with the communication flow, by evaluating the communication correspondence between the server and the nodes. We propose a classification of the communication flow in the previous client-server model in Figure 2. As future work, we plan to extend this communication diagram in a taxonomy classification by uniquely defining its corresponding sub-blocks.

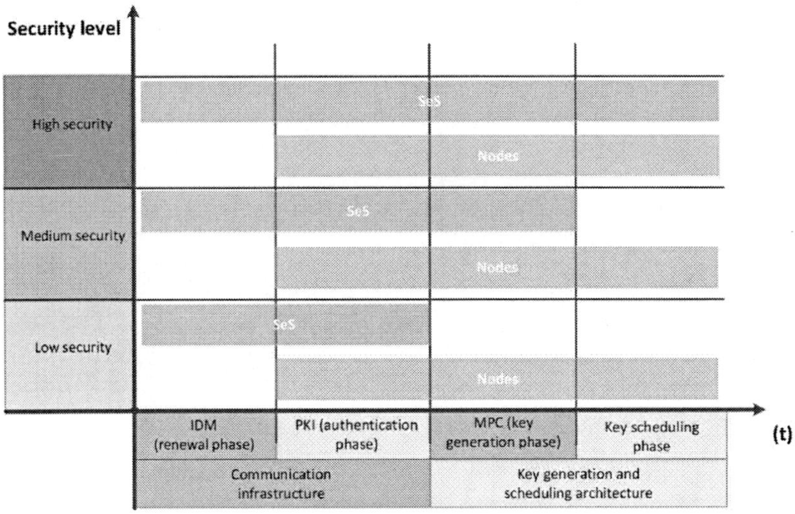

Figure 2: Proposed classification of the communication flow.

ACKNOWLEDGEMENTS

The work of the third author was carried out during the tenure of an ERCIM "Alain Bensoussan" Fellowship Programme. The research leading to these results has received funding from the European Union Seventh Framework Programme (FP7/2007-2013) under grant agreement no. 246016.

REFERENCES

[1] E. Revell, "Method for generating an encryption/decryption key," US Patent Application US 2012/0 087 495 A1, 04 12, 2012.

[2] A. Hudic, E. Revell, and D. E. Simos, "A generation method of cryptographic keys for enterprise communication systems," in 8th International Workshop on Frontiers in Availability, Reliability, and Security (FARES2013), held in conjuction with the 8th International Conference on Availability, Reliability and Security (ARES2013), pp. 406-411, 2013.

[3] W. Stallings, Cryptography and network security - principles and practice (3. ed.). Prentice Hall, 2003.

CROSS-PLATFORM MOBILE APPLICATION DEVELOPMENT

André Nitze and Andreas Schmietendorf
Department of Cooperative Studies, Berlin School of Economics and Law
Berlin, Germany
{andre.nitze, andreas.schmietendorf}@hwr-berlin.de

1. Introduction

Mobile applications have become an important part of our everyday life. May organizations are offering apps to customers and employees to increase retention and productivity [1]. But investment decisions are still a challenge regarding the unprecedented diversity of the mobile market. Smartphone vendors steadily improve the hardware and software of their products resulting in a plethora of device configurations – even within a specific vendor's ecosystem. This causes severe problems for the software engineering discipline and general IT management. Multiple development teams (one for each platform) have to produce and maintain different codebases for one product. Cross-platform mobile applications could be a viable solution to this. The idea of *one* application running on all platforms (e.g. iOS, Android, Windows Phone, Symbian, Bada, webOS) is compelling since development and maintenance efforts would decrease considerably. Analysts predict that more than half of the mobile apps will be hybrid by 2016 [2]. In this work we describe our practical experiences with the current state-of-the-art of cross-platform app development and explain why enterprises should now begin to think about shifting their own or suppliers' mobile software development approaches.

2. Background

Cross-platform applications hinge on a single consistent codebase promising less development and maintenance effort, more focused development expertise and thus a more flexible approach for creating software products. The available technological options for developing cross-platform mobile applications are *web-based* apps and *hybrid* apps. *Web-based apps* (or 'web apps') are basically web sites, which are optimized for mobile devices. Because of this, they are said to lack device specific functionality and performance [3, 4]. Whereas performance issues are slowly decreasing due to optimizations, missing functionality is not an option for today's sensor-packed mobile devices. As opposed to this, *hybrid apps*, though also relying on standardized web technologies, are bundled within a native app "container", which serves as a bridge to access device hardware and functions like vibrating, notifications, camera, GPS sensor and accelerometer. The web standards mainly used are JavaScript for business logic and HTML5 and CSS3 for presentation (styling, transitions etc.) and offline storage. These technologies are used by most modern web browsers and therefore are supported more and more completely by all vendors [5]. As a result of the web technology-based approach, cross-platform apps also circumvent the vendor-specific development process (special programming languages and IDEs).

A recent tech-demo covering core features of Facebook impressively showed that web standards can be used to create a competitive user experience, outperforming even their native counterpart [6] while there also have been less dynamic approaches [7]. This, of course, poses challenges on the programming language used, as it has to provide a high-level API to access all or at least the most commonly used functions of all target platforms (e.g. I/O operations, geolocation and taking pictures). Another important issue concerning cross-platform apps seems to be a divergence in terms of user interface and its challenges [8, 9]. The vendors provide app style guides to the developers to enhance the user experience on their platform through common icon sets, navigation elements, app behavior et cetera. Figure 1 illustrates these differences regarding the navigation approaches in Android and iOS. But even in popular productive apps these style guides are not always applied correctly (e.g. "Deutsche Bahn Navigator").

3. Method

To assess the maturity of the cross-platform app development process we developed a hybrid app prototype. We decided to use the "Sencha Touch" framework because it combines the popular JavaScript framework "ExtJS" and vendor presets to provide a native look and feel on all devices. There are "fallbacks" to provide older devices with full functionality and it utilizes the model-view-controller (MVC) design pattern to foster separation of concerns. The app should provide basic information on a conference: a list of speakers, a time schedule, a floor plan and an activity feed showing recent conference-related tweets. These functions require typical external and internal data access and user interaction.

The objective is to have one codebase to deploy mobile applications to every major mobile operating system from. The "packaging", i.e. creating a container that works as native app on the target platform, is done using the framework's command line interface (CLI). Other ways to wrap the app for multiple platforms include manual packaging via "PhoneGap" (based on Apache Cordova [9]) and the Cloud-based service "PhoneGap Build"[10] .

4. Results

The app has successfully been developed with a common text editor, the CLI and a web browser for testing. The application code has been packaged for Android using the CLI and the most recent Android software development kit (SDK). The cloud-based build was still prone to (undebuggable) errors. The resulting app (see Figure 2) has successfully been tested on two Android-based smartphones (Galaxy Nexus and Samsung S3 Mini) and several modern desktop web browsers (Windows 7: Chrome 26, Internet Explorer 9/10, Firefox 11). It started up fast, ran smoothly (including remote data fetching) and the interaction felt "native".

Figure 1: Hybrid app prototype on a Galaxy Nexus on Android 4.2.2

5. Discussion

The hybrid development approach helped to create a codebase which is usable across multiple platforms. We assume, that if a corresponding user interface is provided for every platform, end-users will not even notice the difference between native and hybrid apps. Though our prototype offers good performance, it does not look "native". Without further customization it imitates Apple's user interface style. Although the app can be themed according to the target platform to further incorporate the different OS's looks and approaches to navigation and user guidance, there is still effort needed to make a hybrid app look and feel like a native app on all platforms. Although there are design commonalities, a common cross-platform style guide for mobile applications is as unlikely to occur as it would be useful. Despite these issues, cross-platform development for mobile devices is picking up pace. Relying on a single codebase, the presented application can be extended, maintained and deployed easily on all platforms. Thus there is more time for platform-specific customization resulting in a more engaging user experience and hence more business value.

6. Conclusions

We learned that hybrid apps indeed are competitive to native apps. We support the opinion that hybrid apps will be pivotal in cross-platform development. That is why organizations should now begin to think about the benefits of cross-platform app development to safeguard their software development investments through a single codebase, more focused professionals and the ability to cover a significant share of the mobile market with their apps.

REFERENCES

[1] IDC Central Europe GmbH, "Managing Mobile Enterprises," 2012. [Online]. Available: http://www.computerwoche.de/fileserver/idgwpcw/files/2137.pdf. [Accessed 16 04 2013].

[2] Gartner Inc., "Gartner Recommends a Hybrid Approach for Business-to-Employee Mobile Apps," 16 04 2016. [Online]. Available: http://www.gartner.com/newsroom/id/2429815. [Accessed 20 04 2016].

[3] M. Korf and E. Oksman, "Native, HTML5, or Hybrid: Understanding Your Mobile Application Development Options," developerforce, 2012. [Online]. [Accessed 21 04 2013].

[4] H. Pearce, "Why native apps remain unrivalled by web apps in user experience and discoverability," 14 02 2013. [Online]. Available: http://www.trademob.com/why-native-apps-remain-unrivalled-by-web-apps-in-user-experience-and-discoverability/. [Accessed 20 04 2013].

[5] Sights Inc., "HTML5 Test," 2013. [Online]. Available: http://html5test.com/. [Accessed 15 05 2013].

[6] J. Avins and J. Nguyen, "The Making of Fastbook: An HTML5 Love Story," 17 December 2015. [Online]. Available: http://www.sencha.com/blog/the-making-of-fastbook-an-html5-love-story. [Accessed 01 05 2013].

[7] B. Peischl, M. Ziefle and A. Holzinger, "A Mobile Information System for Improved Navigation in Public Transport - User Centered Design, Development, Evaluation and e-Business Scenarios of a Mobile Roadmap Application," in Proceedings of the International Conference on e-Business, Rome, Setubal, 2012.

[8] A. Holzinger, M. Geier and P. Germanakos, "On the development of smart adaptive user interfaces for mobile e-Business applications: Towards enhancing User Experience – some lessons learned," in Proceedings of the International Conference on e-Business, Rome, Setubal, 2012.

[9] Apache Foundation, "Apache Cordova," 2013. [Online]. Available: http://cordova.apache.org/. [Accessed 15 05 2013].

[10] Adobe, "Adobe PhoneGap Build," 2013. [Online]. Available: https://build.phonegap.com. [Accessed 15 05 2013].

SHERLOCK: A TOOL PROTOTYPE FOR CHANGE-BASED REGRESSION TESTING

Christian Salomon, Georg Buchgeher, Rudolf Ramler
Software Competence Center Hagenberg GmbH
Hagenberg, Austria
{firstname.lastname}@scch.at

Michael Lusser
OMICRON electronics GmbH
Klaus, Austria
michael.lusser@omicron.at

Abstract
After changing a software system it is difficult, especially for inexperienced testers, to identify regression tests that ensure correct behavior and reveal unwanted side effects. In this paper we present which approaches fits best to our needs when implementing tool support for regresssion testers and our experiences during that time.

1. Introduction

"Change is continual" is the first of the five laws by Lehman and Belady [9] that characterize the dynamics of program evolution. Changes to the software often cause unexpected side effects and inconsistencies with other parts of the software. Regression testing is the re testing of a software system after changes have been made to ensure that the new version of the system has retained the capabilities of the old version and that no new defects have been introduced [1]. While regression testing is an essential and valuable quality assurance measure, it is also a time consuming and costly activity [7]. The involved effort and costs can be reduced by concentrating primarily on those tests, which exercise the parts of the system that have been changed or that are affected by changes. However, selecting a minimal relevant set of regression tests is challenging as it requires in-depth knowledge about the system's implementation to spot all direct and indirect dependencies between the changes made in development and the related test cases that should be re-executed.

We have developed a tool-based approach that assists in selecting regression tests based on data about changes provided by versioning systems and data about dependency extracted from the system's implementation. It is able to support manual regression testing [3] as well as automated model-based testing [6]. The approach has been developed together with the software testing department of OMICRON electronics GmbH. OMICRON develops software solutions for the electrical power industry. The regression testing approach has been evaluated on a large software system that has a development history of more than 15 years. Over these years the system has grown tremendously in size as well as in complexity. Today it consists of more than 2.5 million lines of code (MLOC) and includes the contributions of many different developers, architects, product owners and testers. With the continuous growth of the system also the amount of dependencies between the different modules and layers of the system has increased considerably. Thus, one of the foremost challenges of effective and efficient regression testing lies in achieving and managing the knowledge about dependencies in the software system.

The contributions of our work are, first, an approach for change-based regression testing that integrates the knowledge about changes and dependencies from different viewpoints and sources of the development lifecycle. Second, the approach has been implemented as a tool prototype named Sherlock, which complements OMICON's test and development tool landscape. Third, we present the results from evaluating the proposed approach together with the test team of OMICRON and share our lessons learned from developing and establishing the tool support in context of a large industrial project. Finally, our work may also be of particular interest for practitioners and researchers taking part at the ASQT conference as it can serve as an example of a successful research transfer project between academia and industry using action research [2] to foster continuous feedback and experience exchange in both directions.

2. Approach and Tool Support

A wide range of approaches for regression test case selection and prioritization have been investigated in empirical research. A comprehensive overview of the related work can be found in the literature reviews published by Yoo and Harman [12] and by Engström, Runeson and Skoglund [5]. An overview of code-based change impact analysis techniques has been provided by Li et al. [10]. Our approach assists testers in the selection of test cases related to changes in the software system. Thus, our work is closely related to test case selection approaches, which deal with the selection of a subset of tests that actually check system modifications [12]. Our implemented approach is a variant of the graph-walk technique [11] in combination with the modification-based technique [4].

The implemented tool prototype Sherlock allows relevant test cases to be proposed automatically for a given set of changes. It supports testers in regression testing after bug fixes and enhancements have been made in development. The testers use Sherlock for identifying test cases related to an individual change (e.g., a bug fix) or for all changes within a specified date range (e.g., all fixes and enhancements combined in a maintenance release). Thereby, the main focus of Sherlock lies in proposing a list of relevant test cases that should be included when compiling a regression test suite in the test management system. For identifying relevant test cases, Sherlock incorporates information about changes is retrieved from versioning systems like Subversion or the Microsoft Team Foundation Server, information about which test cases are related to these changes is extracted from code coverage analysis results produced in previous test runs, and dependencies between different parts of the code that are collected with static analysis tools.

3. Results and Lessons Learned

The approach and the tool prototype have been developed in close cooperation with the testing department of OMICRON electronics GmbH. Throughout development the approach and the tool support were evaluated, discussed and enhanced on a regular basis. In addition, the benefit of the tool support was assessed in a workshop by comparing the performance and accuracy of (a) the regression test suite compiled by a tester from the list of test cases proposed by Sherlock with (b) the regression test suites produced by four testers manually selecting relevant test cases, i.e., our control group. The study was based on two major components of the analyzed software project with an overall set of about 400 specified regression test cases. Eight code changes related to bug fixes including bug and fix descriptions were selected from the versioning system. We found that the tester who used Sherlock was able produce test suites with less or equal effort and with the same level of accuracy as the testers in the control group, even when they had detailed knowledge about the selected change. (The control group included the tester who initially found and described the bugs that led to the selected change.) Furthermore, we found that Sherlock performed significantly better in terms of time and accuracy than the junior testers who had no detailed knowledge about the tested modules, in some cases even when the initial list of automatically proposed test cases was not further reduced. Overall we found that Sherlock provides a significant benefit in regression testing when the involved testers lack the necessary background and information about the changes and the affected modules of the software system. Experienced testers find the tool support useful to verify and enhance a manually compiled test suite with the automatically proposed list of tests.

While we were able to continuously improve our approach and to obtain successful first results, we also encountered several challenges and open issues, which we consider of general importance when establishing test case selection in practice. The key lessons we derived from these challenges and issues are as follows. (1) Dependencies between subsystems and modules are highly relevant for regression testing to expose possible latent side effects. However, static analysis approaches are not able to reveal all dependencies relevant for test case selection, e.g., because of multi-language interoperability or reflection mechanisms. (2) Typically, versioning tools provide insufficient information for change analysis as changes are only associated to the modified lines in source code files but not to the affected classes or methods. (3) Some tools, like Microsoft's Visual Studio 2010, provide built-in support for test impact analysis (TIA) [8] at the level of automatically executable integration and unit tests but fall short in support for manual regression tests at system level. (4) Code coverage footprints reveals what parts of the code is executed by a test, but they do not reflect what results and properties are actually checked by this test. Thus, two or more test cases may have an identical footprint but may differ in what aspects of the functionality they verify. Code coverage information alone is not sufficient to determine the relevant tests in such a situation. (5) A major part of the implementation is already executed at system startup phase. Code coverage information collected during this phase has to be excluded from coverage footprints. (6) Finally, keeping code coverage information for manual test cases up-to-date requires a costly manual re-execution of these test cases, which can partly diminish the initial benefits of a change-based regression test approach.

REFERENCES

[1] Ammann, P. and Offutt, J., *Introduction to Software Testing* (1 ed.). Cambridge University Press, 2008.

[2] Avison, D.E., Lau, F., Myers, M.D., and Nielsen, P.A.,Action research. Commun. ACM 42, 1 (January 1999), 94-97, 1999.

[3] Buchgeher, G., Ernstbrunner, C., Ramler, R., and Lusser, M., Towards Tool-Support for Test Case Selection in Manual Regression Testing. In Proc.of the 2013 Testing: Academic & Industrial Conference: Practice and Research Techniques (TAICPART 2013), 2013.

[4] Chen, Y.-F., Rosenblum, D.S., and Vo., K.-P., TestTube: a system for selective regression testing. In Proceedings of the 16th international conference on Software engineering (ICSE '94), 1994.

[5] Engström, E., Runeson, P., and Skoglund, M., A systematic review on regression test selection techniques. Inf. Softw. Technol. 52, 1 (January 2010), 14-30, 2010.

[6] Entin, V., Winder, M., Zhang, B., and Christmann, S., Combining Model-Based and Capture-Replay Testing Techniques of Graphical User Interfaces: An Industrial Approach. In *Proceedings of the 2011 IEEE Fourth International Conference on Software Testing, Verification and Validation Workshops* (ICSTW '11), 2011.

[7] Juergens, E., Regression Test Selection of Manual System Tests in Practice. In Proceedings of the 2011 15th European Conference on Software Maintenance and Reengineering (CSMR '11), 2011.

[8] Laqab, D., and Varcak, T., Streamline Testing Process with Test Impact Analysis. MSDN Library, Microsoft Visual Studio 2010. (http://msdn.microsoft.com/en-us/library/ff576128.aspx), 2010.

[9] Lehmann, M. M., *Program Evolution: Processes of Software Change*. Academic Press Prof, 1985.

[10] Li, B., Sun, X., Leung, H., and Zhang, S., A survey of code-based change impact analysis techniques. Software Test. Verif. Reliab., doi: 10.1002/stvr.1475, 2012.

[11] RothemeL, G., and Harrold, M.J., A safe, efficient regression test selection technique. ACM Trans. Softw. Eng. Methodol. 6, 2 (April 1997), 173-210, 1997.

[12] Yoo, S., and Harmann, M., Regression Testing Minimisation, Selection, and Prioritisation: A Survey. Software Test. Verif. Reliab, vol. 22, iss. 2, pp. 67-120., 2012.

TESTING IN THE SERVICE ORIENTED ARCHITECTURE

Seema Jehan, Ingo Pill, and Franz Wotawa
Institute for Software Technology, Graz University of Technology
Inffeldgasse 16b/II
8010 Graz, Austria
{seema.jehan, ingo.pill, franz.wotawa}@ist.tuGraz.at

Abstract
Despite doubts and security concerns from the verification and testing community, Service Oriented Architecture has revolutionized the today's computing. The distributed, asynchronous and dynamic nature of SOA paradigm makes traditional testing and verification methods a daunting task. Hence, this new wave of change in computing demands new testing methodologies to better cope with the challenges faced by the SOA. BPEL is a standard workflow language used for the modeling of business processes by the composition of various heterogeneous web services. This paper describes recent work on the testing of BPEL compositions based on symbolic execution and contract based testing.

1. Introduction

SOA is an architectural style, which laid foundation for wide range of software models and technologies such as Software as a Service and Web Services. We use BPEL to describe SOAs. It is used for the orchestration of multiple distributed and heterogeneous web services to realize a business workflow.

The problem of devising testing methodology for BPEL composition has been previously explored, but suffers from lack of empirical results[1]. BPEL processes have just interface description of the invoked web services, which raises the issue of "TRUST" in such complex business scenarios[3]. That means, we can never be sure that web services are implemented as described in the interfaces. That makes the testing of BPEL compositions grey box, whereupon the BPEL processes can be unit tested but the web services are black box. For that reason, we propose a solution based on pre- and post conditions to reason about the behavior of these external web services.

Primarily, three approaches have been discussed for the model based testing of BPEL compositions i.e. *symbolic execution, petri nets* and *model checking*[3]. We use graph-based approach based on the symbolic execution. Yuan[2] has also proposed the similar approach earlier. Our work differs from them in a way that after generating test paths using path coverage criterion, we further augment these paths using pre- and post conditions. These conditions are specified using the BPEL expression language. The quality of the test suite is judged by different coverage metrics i.e. activity, branch coverage and the mutation score. For that purpose, we make use of the Unit testing tool[5] and the mutation testing[6]. The business process is first deployed on the BPEL engine and the web services are tested using the generated test suite.

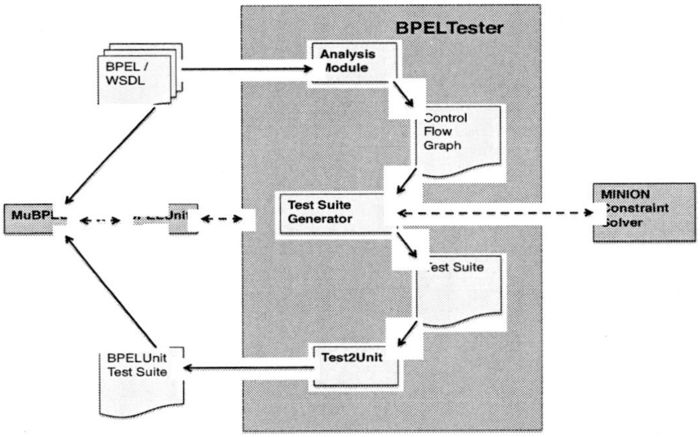

Figure 1: The BPELTester Architecture

2. Test Case Generation

The general overview of the architecture is shown in the fig1. The tool is implemented in Java and has three components i.e. *analysis module, test suite generator* and the *test2unit*. The Analysis module takes the BPEL artifacts and converts them into a control flow graph. The resulting flow graph might be augmented using pre- and post conditions. The second module, test suite generator performs two main functions i.e. first, it derives the test paths between the selected nodes in the graph. Second, it checks the feasibility of obtained paths using the constraint solver *MINION*[7].If a particular path is a feasible, this would represent a valid test case. The required input and the expected output of the test case are obtained from the constraint solver. The detailed description of the conversion of each test path into constraint representation is presented in our previous work[4]. The last module, Test2Unit is responsible for generating executable test suite, which is compatible with the unit and mutation-testing tool.

3. Initial results

The current focus of the research has been on the evaluation of the mutation testing for the generated test suite. The mutation testing is based on introducing faults in the original program. The altered version of the original program is called a "mutant". If a test suite differentiates the altered program from the original one, then it is called a killed mutant. The larger the number of killed mutants, the better is the quality of the test suite. For the initial results, we have considered five small case studies comprising of synchronous, executable BPEL processes. The examples used included both the basic activities such as *receive*, *reply*, *assign* and *invoke* but also the structured activities like *if*, *while* and *sequence*. The obtained results regarding activity, branch coverage and mutation with respect to the path length of a rather complex example ATM are presented in the Figure 2. The empirical results are encouraging, as we obtained 100 % activity and branch coverage for the minimum number of paths. The killed mutants could only reach up to 90% and afterwards it stabilizes. The time needed to generate the test suite was less than a second. But, larger business processes still need to be considered for the better estimation of the usefulness of our approach.

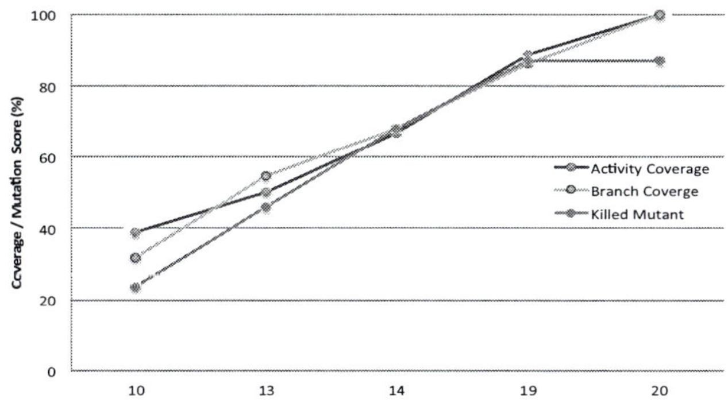

Figure 2: Coverage and mutation score vs. path length for the ATM

4. Conclusions

The contribution of our current research is twofold. First, we derive test suite for BPEL compositions using constraint and contract based testing. Using contracts on the web services invocation would help in diagnosing the malfunctioning of the web services. Second, we evaluate the effectiveness of the generated test suite using different coverage metrics like activity, branch and mutation. The initial results obtained provide sound foundation for the further research. Particularly, we are interested in the test suite generation of the asynchronous processes in the future. For the failing test cases, we plan to include the diagnosis engine. Another key area of research would be to include the non-functional requirements in the test generation process.

REFERENCES

[1] Z. Zakaria, R. Atan, A. A. A. Ghani, and N. F. M. Sani, "Unit testing approaches for bpel: A systematic review," in *16th Asia- Pacific Software Engineering Conference*. IEEE Computer Society, 2009, pp. 316–322.

[2] Z. L. Yuan Yuan and W. Sun, "A graph-search based approach to bpel4ws test generation," in *Software Engineering Advances, International Conference on,* Oct. 2006, p. 14.

[3] M. H. Mustafa Bozkurt and Y. Hassoun, "Testing web services: A survey," Department of Computer Science, King's College London, Tech. Rep. TR-10-01, January 2010.

[4] S. Jehan, I. Pill, and F. Wotawa, "Functional soa testing based on constraints," in *8th International Workshop on Automation of Software Test,* 2013, to appear.

[5] D. Lu˙bke, "Bpel unit," 2006. [Online]. Available: http://bpelunit.github.com

[6] "Mubpel- a mutation testing tool for ws-bpel." [Online]. Available: https://neptuno.uca.es/redmine/projects/sources-fm/wiki/MuBPEL

[7] I. P. Gent, C. Jefferson, and I. Miguel, "Minion: A fast scalable constraint solver," in *In: Proceedings of ECAI 2006, Riva del Garda*. IOS Press, 2006, pp. 98–102

WITH STANDARD SOFTWARE ON THE SAFE SIDE? TESTING OF STANDARD SOLUTIONS

Renate Weichselbraun
ANECON Software Design und Beratung GmbH
Alser Straße 4 / Hof 1
1090 Vienna, Austria
renate.weichselbraun@anecon.com

1. Initial Situation

Do you know this situation:
Your Company has decided to buy standard software e.g. a new ERP system, payroll accounting, a system for the production control or a central document management system? You have planned a particular development and testing budged for the integration in your existing system landscape. Nevertheless, you are faced with the situation that a self-evident functionality is not operating as expected and the test budged is no longer sufficient?

The use of standard software is a tempting alternative to individually developed applications for many companies. Lower costs are often called as the main advantage but in fact they become relative because of a required adaption/configuration to existing system components.

2. Standard software is not automatic free of errors

There is no standard software, which supports all processes of an organization without an individual adjustment. The costs of integration, configuration and adjustment will be realized but the impact on purchased software and the changed system landscape are underestimated. Even with just small changes or configurations you have to expect significant side effects.

The risks of necessary adjustments at the standard software are not transparent. In many cases, supplier contracts not even include clear responsibilities or acceptance criteria.

It is also important to have a big picture of your system landscape. If you do not know your requirements, how can you choose the best solution for your business?

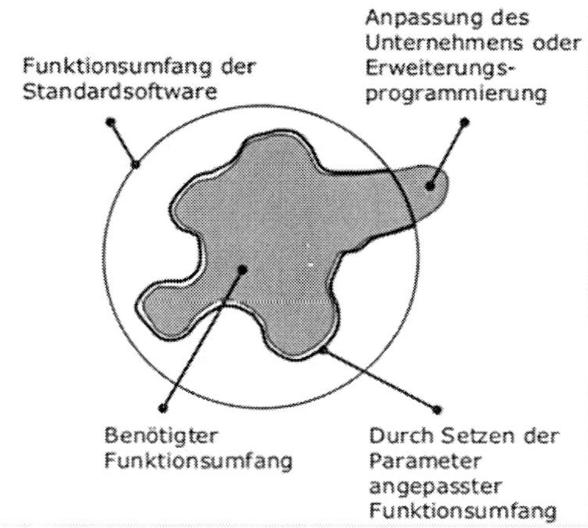

Figure 1: © 2008-2012,
Lehrstuhl für Wirtschaftsinformatik, Europa-Universität Viadrina Frankfurt

3. Conclusion

The focuses of testing standard solutions are on *system integration tests* and acceptance tests. A good system integration test protects from unexpected costs or postponements.

It is necessary to *involve quality assurance measurements as early as possible*. The expected functionality of the entire system is ensured by prioritizing defined and *measurable acceptance criteria*. Ideally, these acceptance criteria are agreed by contract.

The effort for *data migration tests* is often underestimated. Data migration gives you the chance, to clean up data. But this needs time and the knowledge of the experts – which data are correct and which one are still needed?

Efficient regression testing is an essential factor for success in every test project. In implementation projects this fact often gets underestimated. With every new version you need to make sure that all previously worked still works.

The initiation of standard software is an IT project and therefore should be *set up as an IT project*. A realistic planning and an appropriate project-approach make a significant contribution to a successful implementation.

ALIGNING SOFTWARE ENGINEERING ACTIVITIES WITH BUSINESS NEEDS AND STRATEGY: SCALABLE PRODUCT MANAGEMENT PROCESSES FOR HIGH-QUALITY, SUSTAINABLE PRODUCTS

Fritz Stallinger
Software Competence Center Hagenberg, Process and Quality Engineering,
Softwarepark 21, A-4232 Hagenberg
fritz.stallinger@scch.at

Robert Schossleitner
STIWA Automation GmbH,
Salzburger Straße 52, A-4800 Attnang-Puchheim
robert.schossleitner@stiwa.com

1. Motivation, Goals, and Approach

Software development organizations are more and more confronted with the need to develop, maintain and enhance their software as a product (cf. e.g. [7]). The implied transition towards a product-oriented enterprise causes a change in the whole organization, requires the consideration of the views of additional stakeholders, and puts the focus to business and market considerations, additionally to technological ones.

A key goal in such a transition is to harvest the benefits of pre-defined or pre-developed products or product components while still meeting individual customers' or market needs. To fully exploit the potential of the therefore necessary product- and reuse-focused development approaches and to foster the development of sustainable products and underlying assets, core software engineering activities like requirements or architecture engineering have to be closely aligned with strategic and economic product aspects that are typically related to – and ideally derived from – the overall business goals of the organization. Software product management is expected to provide exactly this link and integrate business and product related goals with core software engineering activities.

In this context, the long-term vision of our work is to enable and support the transition of software development organizations towards product-oriented development by providing guidance in terms of reference processes and best practices for establishing software product management as key intermediary between business-related aspects and proper software engineering activities.

The underlying approach focuses on identifying the key activities related to software product management and their interplay with business and engineering functions in order to foster the collaborative and scalable implementation of software product management, independent from sophisticated and overburdening role descriptions or scarce key personnel. The cornerstones of the work developing and validating this approach have been presented to the process improvement and product line engineering communities (cf. [5, 6, 7, 8]) and are sketched in the following.

2. Activity-oriented Analysis of Product Management Frameworks

A selection of frameworks available for product management and partly product engineering (cf. [2, 3, 4, 9]) has been analyzed with respect to involved activities. They all have distinct and diverse foci, are often linked with specific development paradigms, and lack completeness and integration with core engineering activities. Similarly, the models underlying traditional software process improvement approaches, e.g. ISO/IEC 12207 on software life cycle processes [1], generally lack the provision of explicit or detailed software product management practices. The results of this analysis and comparison with ISO/IEC 12207 are sketched in *Table 1* (cf. [8] for details).

Table 1. Software product management key activities, source frameworks, and coverage by ISO/IEC 12207.

	Source Frameworks				Coverage by ISO/IEC 12207 Error! Reference source not found.
Key Software Product Management Activities	**v. de Weerd et al.** Error! Reference source not found.	**SEI** Error! Reference source not found.	**Pohl et al.** Error! Reference source not found.	**MSF** Error! Reference source not found.	
Product Portfolio Management	•		•		Partly
Product Life Cycle Management	•		•		Fully
Product Roadmapping	•	•	•		None
Release Planning	•			•	None
Product Planning	•	•	•	•	None
Product Controlling		•	•		Partly
Market Monitoring	•	•	•	•	None
Customer Interface Management	•	•	•		Partly
Funding		•			None
Product Innovation			•		None
Cross-functional Communication				•	Partly
Requirements Engineering & Management	•	•			Largely
Domain and Product Line Scoping	•	•	•		Largely
Asset Identification	•	•			Fully

3. Distillation of Software Product Management Practices

Building on these results, a best practice based process reference model for software product management has been developed that can be applied stand-alone as well as integrated with ISO/IEC 12207 [1]. The model is presented in detail in [5]. *Figure 1* illustrates the structure of the model. The model is comprised of 13 processes grouped into three process categories:

- The *Software Product Management Processes* category comprises the core product management and product planning processes.
- The *Software Product Management Support Processes* category comprises the processes that support any of the other processes in the reference model.
- The *Software Engineering Lifecycle Processes* category comprises the core engineering processes interfering with product management.

4. Initial Validation

The emerging reference model has been validated in a case study (cf. [6]). The goal of this initial pilot application has been to validate the proposed model with respect to its applicability, completeness, clarity, etc., to identify respective enhancements and improvements to the model, and to confirm its potential to help identify improvements to software product management.

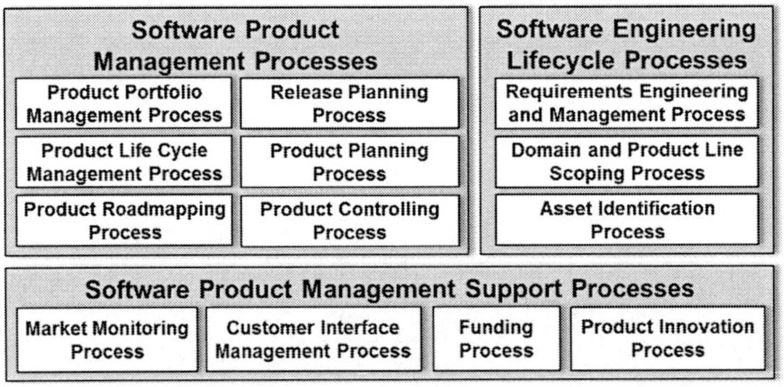

Figure 1: Software Product Management Reference Processes.

The feedback from the assessed organization and the assessors confirmed a satisfactory level of clarity and understandability of the model element descriptions, a high completeness, satisfactory applicability, and the capability of the model to identify business-relevant improvements.

REFERENCES

[1] International Standards Organization, ISO/IEC 12207:2008: Systems and software engineering - Software life cycle processes, International Standards Organization 2008.

[2] Microsoft DevelopeR Network, Microsoft Solutions Framework, available at: http://msdn.microsoft.com/de-de/library/bb979125.aspx, last accessed: February 24, 2014.

[3] PohL, K., Böckle, G., van der Linden, F., Software Product Line Engineering – Foundations, Principles, and Techniques, Springer, Berlin 2005.

[4] Software Engineering Institute, A Framework for Software Product Line Practice, Version 5.0, available at: http://www.sei.cmu.edu/productlines/frame_report/index.html, last accessed: February 24, 2014.

[5] Stallinger, F., Neumann, R., Extending ISO/IEC 12207 with Software Product Management: A Process Reference Model Proposal, in: A. Mas, A. Mesquida, T. Rout, R. V. O'Connor, A. Dorling (Eds), Software Process Improvement and Capability Determination, 12th International Conference, SPICE 2012, Palma, Spain, May 2012, Proceedings, Communications in Computer and Information Science, vol. 290, pp. 93-106, Springer, Heidelberg 2012.

[6] Stallinger, F., Neumann, R., Schossleitner, R., Assessing Software Product Management Capability: An Industry Validation Case Study, in: T. Woronowicz et al. (Eds.), Software Process Improvement and Capability Determination, 13th International Conference, SPICE 2013, Bremen, Germany, June 2013, Proceedings, Communications in Computer and Information Science, vol. 349, pp. 95-106, Springer, Berlin Heidelberg 2013.

[7] Stallinger, F., Neumann, R., Schossleitner, R., Kriener, S., Migrating Towards Evolving Software Product Lines: Challenges of an SME in a Core Customer-driven Industrial Systems Engineering Context, Second International Workshop on Product Line Approaches in Software Engineering (PLEASE 2011), May 22-23, 2011, Waikiki, Honolulu, HI, USA, Proceedings, ACM ISBN: 978-1-4503-0584-6, pp. 15-19.

[8] Stallinger, F., Neumann, R., SchossleitneR, R., Zeilinger, R., Linking Software Life Cycle Activities with Product Strategy and Economics: Extending ISO/IEC 12207 with Product Management Best Practices, in: R. V. O'Connor, T. Rout, F. McCaffery, A. Dorling (Eds.), Software Process Improvement and Capability Determination, 11th International Conference, SPICE 2011, Dublin, Ireland, May/June 2011, Proceedings, Communications in Computer and Information Science, vol. 155, pp. 157-168, Springer, Berlin Heidelberg 2011.

[9] van de Weerd, I., Brinkkemper, S., Nieuwenhuis, R., Versendaal, J., Bijlsma, L., Towards a Reference Framework for Software Product Management, in: 14th IEEE International Requirements Engineering Conference, pp. 319-322, IEEE Computer Society, Minneapolis/ST. Paul, Minnesota, USA 2006.

ADOPTING AGILE WITH CONTINUOUS INTEGRATION TO EXCEL IN SOFTWARE DEVELOPMENT[2]

Elisabeth Richter, Wolfgang Richter
JIPP.IT GmbH
Neugasse 111
8200 Gleisdorf, Austria
wolfgang.richter@jipp.it, elisabeth.richter@jipp.it

1. Introduction - Adopting Agile with Continuous Integration to excel in software development

The software market is often described as increasingly demanding and fast moving. Software is outdated extremely fast. Changing markets or new government regulations force organizations and thereby their software vendors to react quickly. Many software development companies struggle to finish their software development endeavours with satisfactory results for their customers.

In many companies problems in one project cascade into problems in subsequent projects. Additionally, most projects are staffed with too little employees, resulting in an unevenly distributed workload and troubles with resource scheduling. As a countermeasure companies decide to introduce agile methods and an adoption attempt started. These adoption processes are often unstructured and a responsible person was not assigned. Consequently, results become meagre and discouraging.

2. Challenges alongside adoption

The adoption of agile methods and Continuous Integration is not an easy endeavour. It has to be dealt with scepticism from employees and customers. Some practices seem counterintuitive at first and are rejected. Consequently, the person responsible for the adoption process has to act tactfully but with emphasis. Approaches from change management can ease the adoption process.

The adoption is further complicated, if the context of the organization is not originally ready for agility. Hence, in addition to the adoption of agile methods a part of or the entire organization has to be reorganized.

Often one team works at multiple projects concurrently. Agile methods emphasize one team – one project, hence a restructuring of ongoing projects needs to start in parallel.

Increased coordination effort and inhomogeneous sprints may slow down progress or even cancel out benefits. In conclusion, the adoption of agile methods and Continuous Integration requires companies to invest some effort to avoid pitfalls and utilize their special approach best.

---

[2] Derived from a master thesis of 2010 at the Technical University Graz [4].

3. Goals for adoptions

Based on the most frequently appearing issues and challenges in adoptions four main goals can be derived:

- Increased customer satisfaction through improved reliability and adherence to delivery dates.
- Earlier project completion through improved project progress and control to optimize cost and payment situation.
- Broadened documentation of decisions and lessons.
- Increased empowerment of each employee.

To achieve listed goals two main fields of operation can be identified. First, the organization and projects are to be analysed to determine the situation at hand. Then, the specific areas of improvement and demands on methods are to be derived. As a common conclusion, an experienced, strong-willed coach should be commissioned to overtake the adoption of agile methods and to select an appropriate set of practices.

Agile software development is simple and complex at the same time, therefore it is hard to reduce it to a few common concepts. Nevertheless, to gain a basic understanding, the core concepts *Iterative and Incremental*, and *Adaptive* are highlighted.

Iterative and Incremental: In simple words, iterative and incremental means delivering a deployable product after a predetermined period of time. The concept of being iterative is rather easy. Basically, it can be compared to a project milestone reoccurring after a fixed, always identical period of time. The de-facto standard for iterations is currently two weeks.

Being incremental is not complex, but often hard to implement. After each iteration, a deployable software product based on the last increment has to be ready. This requires focus on a common goal, appropriate planning, technical excellence and practices such as *Continuous Integration* in place.

Adaptive: Adaptability is to be responsive to change. Flexibility and constant and early feedback allows to react according to the current situation and need. Some situations require striking new paths not immediately evident in feedback. For example, ceasing product acceptance might indicate the need for a new product, not a more aggressive marketing strategy. This aspect is often neglected in criticism against agility. [2] sums it up in his favourite description of agility:

"*Agility is the ability to both create and respond to change in order to profit in a turbulent business environment.*"

4. Overcoming the challenge, reaching the goal

A change project with the goal to install an appropriate method and supporting practices needs to be started. Often companies try to start the adoption in parallel to daily business without providing the required infrastructure and resources. This promises failure. A change project for the adoption has to be set up, staffed with the appropriate people, and requires commitment from executives top-down. Once this project is started, practices can be installed, like Continuous Integration.

Continuous Integration: After completing a task the changes are integrated with the whole software. Collisions with other changes and failing tests are fixed. Eventual issues or bugs are at most a day old and therefore easier to find and fix than some created a few weeks ago. Bug tracking can be omitted, since bugs are fixed immediately when they occur. Solutions will be documented [1].

Continuous Integration prevents code-bases from drifting. It requires Configuration Management, which enables team-members to work independently on every part of the code. A Build System transforms source-code into executable code. In addition it runs tests automatically. Each team-member is responsible to integrate changes immediately. Unwanted side-effects can be identified fast and eliminated. Each team-member must not wait longer than a few minutes for the build. Otherwise the risk of omitting builds rises. Longer test-runs should be done only in nightly, automatically run builds. ([1], p. 97-99), ([3], p. 202-203).

5. Results

The adoption of agile methods and Continuous Integration usually contributes to success substantially through

- better control of project and individual features,
- continuous feedback,
- continuous team and process development and
- independency on individual's knowledge.

In software development often a compromise is made between speed and quality, but with excellent, rapid feedback and superb discipline both can be achieved. The agile concepts for rapid feedback are short iterations, release minimum feature sets incrementally, review code and software and plenty of customer communication. Practices for technical feedback are continuous integration and testing on different levels ([3], p. 177ff). A thorough agile adoption strategy gives thought to all parts and members of the organization in change. Along the adoption path all named practices and concepts are considered and implemented and allow for a new hyper productive software development.

REFERENCES

[1] Beck, K., eXtreme Programming explained - Embrace change. Addison-Wesley, Boston et. al. ISBN:201616416.

[2] Highsmith, J., Agile Software Development Ecosystems. The Agile Software Development Series. Addison-Wesley, Boston et.al. ISBN:0201760436.

[3] Poppendieck, M. and Poppendieck, T. (2007). Implementing Lean Software Development -From Concept to Cash. The Addison Wesley Signature Series. Addison-Wesley, Upper Saddle River et. al. ISBN:0321437381.

[4] Richter, E. (2010). Adopting agile software development in a multi-project environment. Master thesis TU Graz, Institute for General Management and Organization.

THE DARK SIDE OF AGILE SOFTWARE DEVELOPMENT, FIRST RESULTS

Andrea Janes, Giancarlo Succi
Freie Universität Bozen
{andrea.janes, giancarlo.succi}@unibz.it

Abstract
Many innovations, we think also Agile Methods, go through Gartner's Hype Cycle. Agile Methods are currently stuck in the "Trough of Disillusionment". We present possible reasons why this is so as well as the "Dark Agile Manifesto", an illustration how Agile Methods are misinterpreted to legitimate hacker behavior. This article presents the feedback of 85 respondents to our questionnaire in which they state if they agree or not with the lines of the "Dark Agile Manifesto."

1. Gartner's Hype Cycle

We have seen many innovations going through a phase of over-enthusiasm or "hype" and then, when the expectations turn out to be unrealistic, to result in a generalized disappointment. New technologies offer new opportunities so the hope to overcome unsettled problems with the existing solutions is high and generates excessively optimistic expectations.

We think that Gartner's Hype Cycle [2] describes well this phenomenon. It encompasses five stages that many innovations go through before becoming productive. Not all innovations manage to reach the fifth stage; some become obsolete before the end.

Figure 1 shows the five phases. The Hype Cycle begins with the technology trigger, an innovation that generates significant attention in field because it solves a significant problem, has the potential to solve a significant problem, or offers new possibilities. An example for such a technology is currently Google Glass[3]. In Gartner's Hype Cycle, this phase culminates in the Peak of Inflated Expectations.

With time, it becomes clear that the excessive expectations cannot be met and so the innovation gets less and less attention and enters the Trough of Disillusionment, it becomes unfashionable. Some continue to use it to further explore its real benefits and in doing this, they may pass through to the Slope of Enlightenment. This final phase, for those technologies that do not become obsolete before reaching it, is the Plateau of Productivity, a phase in which the benefits of the innovation are widely demonstrated and accepted. The final height of the plateau (the visibility of the technology) depends on how applicable the innovation eventually is.

2. The Dark Agile Manifesto

We believe, that Agile has followed the Gartner Hype Cycle and it has now reached the Trough of Disillusionment, where it is currently stuck. We presented the arguments for this belief in an essay during SPLASH 2012 [3], in which we conjectured that this is due to:

[3] Google Glass, http://www.google.com/glass

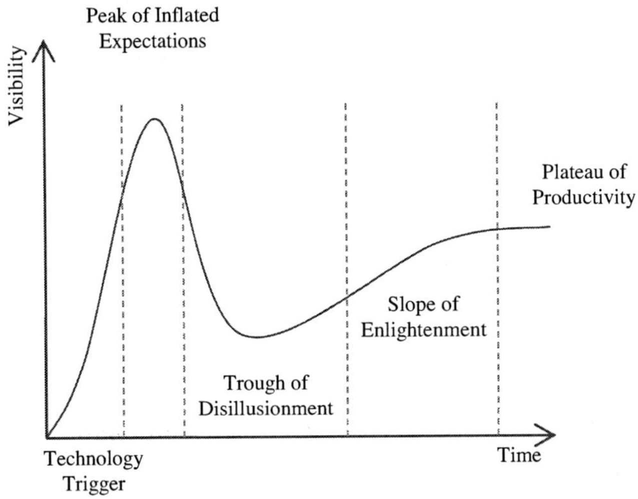

Figure 1: The five phases of Gartner's Hype Cycle [2]

- The wrong expectation that writing software is like building houses: also in construction work, as soon as something completely new has to be built, problems can arise. A prominent example is Berlin's new airport, "named after former Chancellor Willy Brandt, but its construction faults have brought it such infamy that the foundation managing Brandt's political legacy is worried about having the Nobel laureate associated with the project [1]."
- Project managers obtain the wrong training: the Guide to the Project Management Body of Knowledge (PMBOK, American National Institute standard ANSI/PMI 99/001/2008), a recognized standard for the project management profession [4], expects a waterfall-like progression of the different activities of the project. The PMBOK just briefly (a paragraph of 8 lines of text) mentions the possibility to divide the project in project phases and to perform these phases iteratively, but reserves this solution only for "largely undefined, uncertain, or rapidly changing environments such as research [4].
- The term "Agile" is sometimes used to legitimize hacker behavior. We call this the "Dark Side of Agile", which we illustrate modifying the Agile Manifest as in Figure 2.

We further conjectured, that the reason why it is not clear when Agile works and when not, i.e., why Agile is not at the Plateau of Productivity, is that Agile Methods have been conceived and refined by gurus, e.g., Extreme Programming by Kent Beck, Crystal Clear by Alistair Cockburn, and Scrum by Ken Schwaber.

The guru has no advantage in explaining the reasons for his advice, otherwise his or her role as a guru would vanish. In this way, the adopters remain dependent on the guru: the adopters need the guru to continue to use the method in cases not described by the guru up front, e.g., how it can be extended, in which order the different practices should be adopted, etc. One way out of this dilemma is measurement [5], which we further describe in [3].

We are uncovering ~~better~~ **the only** ways of developing
software by doing it and ~~helping~~ **teaching** others do it.
Through this work we have come to value:

Individuals and interactions ~~over~~ **and not** processes and tools
Working software ~~over~~ **and not** comprehensive documentation
Customer collaboration ~~over~~ **and not** contract negotiation
Responding to change ~~over~~ **and not** following a plan

That is, ~~while~~ **since** there is **no** value in the items on
the right, we value **only** the items on the left ~~more~~.

Figure 2: The dark agile manifesto [2]

We created the web site http://darkagilemanifesto.org, through which we ask each visitor to tell us for each line of the dark manifesto, if he or she agrees or not. So far, 85 respondents from 22 different countries, 24 managers, 18 trained professionals, 17 consultants, 12 researchers, 5 self-employed, 7 skilled laborers, 1 administrative worker, and 1 student answered as we depict in Figure 3.

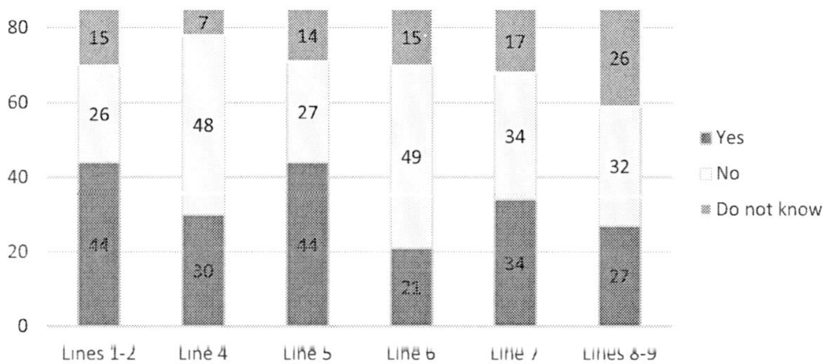

Figure 3: The answers of the first 85 respondents of our questionnaire

In the first results, a majority confirms that proposers of Agile Methods often assume an attitude of a teacher instead of a supporter (lines 1-2) as well as that Agile Methods are often used to promote more focus on the software instead of the documentation (line 5).

REFERENCES

[1] Crossland, D. 2013. Spiegel Online. 'Brandt Would Turn in His Grave': Berlin's Blighted Airport May Need a New Name, http://www.spiegel.de/international/germany/report-casts-doubt-on-berlin-airport-being-named-after-willy-brandt-a-877647.html

[2] Hype Cycle, http://www.gartner.com/technology/research/methodologies/hype-cycle.jsp

[3] Janes, A. and Succi, G. 2012. The dark side of agile software development. In Proceedings of the ACM international symposium on New ideas, new paradigms, and reflections on programming and software (Onward! '12). ACM, New York, NY, USA

[4] Project Management Institute. 2008. A guide to the project management body of knowledge: (PMBOK guide). Project Management Institute, Inc., Newtown Square, PA

[5] Scotto, M., Sillitti, A., Succi G., Vernazza, T. 2006. A non-invasive approach to product metrics collection. Journal of Systems Architecture, Volume 52, Issue 11, North-Holland Publishing

THE ROLE OF THE AGILE TESTER IN DEALING WITH TECHNICAL DEBT

Harry Sneed and Richard Seidl
ANECON Software Design u. Beratung GmbH,
Alser Straße 4 / Hof 1
1090 Vienna, Austria
{harry.sneed, richard.seidl}@anecon.com

1. What is Technical Debt?

"*Technical Debt*", is a term for the work required to put a piece of software in the state that it should be in. It may be that this is never done and the software remains in the substandard state forever, but still the debt remains. In other words, technical debt is a term for substandard software. It was coined to describe poor quality software in terms that business managers can relate to, namely in terms of money, money required to fix a problem [5]. Managers should become aware of the fact the neglect of software quality costs them money and that these costs can be calculated. The notion of "debt" should remind them that someday they have to pay it back or at least try to reduce it. The amount of the national debt can be measured absolutely in terms of Dollars or Euros and relatively in relation to the gross national product. The same applies to the technical debt. It too can be measured absolutely in terms of money required to renovate the software and relatively in terms of the costs of renovation relative to the development costs.
The notion of "*technical debt*" was coined by Ward Cunningham at the OOPSLA conference in 1992. The original meaning as used by Cunningham was "all the not quite right code which we postpone making it right." [2]. With this statement he was referring to the inner quality of the code. Later the term was extended to imply all that should belong to a properly developed software system, but which was purposely left out to remain in time or in budget, system features such as error handling routines, exception conditions, security checks and backup and recovery procedures and essential documents such as the architecture design, the user guide, the data model and the updated requirement specification. All of the many security and emergency features can be left out by the developer and the users will never notice it until a problem comes up. Should someone inquire about them, the developers can always say that these features were postponed to a later release. In an agile development they would say that they were put in the backlog. In his book on "Managing Software Debt - Building for Inevitable Change", Sterling describes how this debt accumulates – one postponement at a time, one compromise after another [7].

2. Measuring Technical Debt

It has always been known that poor coding practices and missing features cause higher maintenance costs but no one has ever put a price tag on it. This has now been done by Bill Curtis and his colleagues from CAST Software Limited in Texas. Their suggestion for computing the costs of bad quality assigns each deficiency type to the effort required to remove it. The basis for their calculation is an experience database from which the average cost of removing each deficiency type is calculated. The data from scores of refactoring projects has been accumulated in this database [3]. For example, the refactoring and retesting of a single overly complex method can cost a half day. Considering an hourly rate of US $70, that leads to a total cost of $280. The cost of a missing exception handling may cost only an hour but if five hundred such handlings are missing the cost will amount to some $35,000. The cost of adding a missing security check can cost up to three person days or $1600. The main contribution of Curtis and his colleagues is that they have identified and classified more than a hundred software problem types and put a price tag on them. Samples of their problem types are:

- Builtin SQL queries (subject to hacking)
- Empty Catch Blocks (no exception handling)
- Overly complex conditions (error prone)
- Missing comments (detracts from comprehension)
- Redundant Code (swells the code amount and leads to maintenance errors)
- Non-uniform variable naming (making the code hard to understand)
- Loops without an emergency brake (can cause system crash)
- Too deeply nested statements (are difficult to change).

The costs of such deficiencies are the sum of the costs for each deficiency type. The cost of each deficiency type is the number of occurrences of that deficiency times the average effort required to remove and retest that deficiency as taken from the experience database. (see Figure 1: Measuring the Amount of Technical Debt)

Technical Debt in Terms of Code Deficiencies

Major deficiencies sorted by number of occurrences	Correction Effort (Person Hours)	
(10) Return Value is not controlled after Method Call 2435	x 0,5	= 1217
(22) Public Variables should be avoided in Classes 2280	x 1	= 2280
(01) IO-Operations are not in a try block 913	x 1,5	= 1370
(25) Class is not derived from a Superordinate Class 219	x ?	= ?
(14) Control logic exceeds maximum allowed nesting level 962	x 2	= 1924
(15) Missing Final clause in method declaration 856	x 0,5	= 428
(04) Data Casting should be avoided 692	x 2	= 1384
(18) Check on incoming public request is missing 535	x 4	= 2140
(26) Nested Classes are not allowed 376	x 4	= 1504
(27) Returning a Function my cause an endless loop 239	x 6	= 1434
(11) Conditions should not contain an Assignment 150	x 1	= 150
(17) Try and Catch clauses do not match 112	x 1	= 112
(13) Default is missing in Switch Statement 85	x 1	= 85
(12) Case block should contain a Break statement 77	x 2	= 154
(08) Method Invocation with Array is not in a try Block 31	x 3	= 93
(07) External Variables are not allowed 29	x 2	= 58
(06) Standard IO Functions are prohibited 21	x 4	= 84
(09) There should be no global Data Definitions in C# 5	x 2	= 10
(02) Two Dimensional Arrays violate 1. Normal Form 2	x 8	= 16
Total Correction Effort		= 14.443

Figure 1: Measuring the Amount of Technical Debt

3. Early Recognition of accumulating Technical Debt

The main contribution of agile testing is to establish a rapid feedback to development [1]. This is the rational for having the testers in the team. When it comes to preventing quality degradation and increasing debt, the testers in an agile project have more to do than just test. They are there to assure the quality of the product at all levels during construction. This should be accomplished through a number of control measures, measures such as reviewing the stories, transforming the stories into testable specifications, reviewing the architectural design, inspecting the code, validating the unit tests, performing continuous integration testing and running an acceptance test with the user. As pointed out by Paul Duvall in his book on Continuous Integration, the best way to detect technical debt is with automated code analysis tools [4]. Within minutes the tester can have all the missing features and code deficiencies listed out in a deficiency report. Provided he has a table for the assignment of effort to the individual deficiencies he can also have the amount of the debt computed. This should be done for each new release as part of the release process.

4. Instigating Measures to reduce Technical Debt

In an agile development project it is up to the tester to see that the technical debt is reduced. He can do this by getting the product owner to make periodic clean-up releases, releases in which no new functionality is added, but only the quality is improved [6]. There are now many refactoring tools available which automatically factor out deeply nested code blocks, split classes, finalize classes, insert breaks, add try/catch clauses and replace hard-wired data. These refactoring runs take only minutes, but it is up to the developer to run them. Other types of deficiencies such as missing security checks, missing error handling, non-standard data names and overly complex conditions have to be corrected manually by the developers. This may take several days. When the improvements have been made, the source modules affected have to run through the unit test again, the components reintegrated and the system test repeated. If the tests are already set up and automated, this will require only a day or too. If not, it can require weeks. This is the main reason why project teams are reluctant to refactor. They are afraid of the retesting effort.
Refactoring and Retesting should not be a problem if the agile development teams are equipped with the proper tools. Much of the quality improvement work can be automated and almost all of the retesting. The tester should only be there to run the tools and to evaluate the results. In this way, technical debt can be brought under control with a minimum of effort.

5. Conclusion

Technical debt is not something that cannot be handled. However projects must be aware of it and its consequences for their product. They should know that if they ignore it, it will someday cause the death of their product. Therefore, they have to monitor and measure it, and in regular intervals work to reduce it. It is the job of the tester to see that this is done.

REFERENCES

[1] Crispin, L. / Gregory, J.: Agile Testing – A practical Guide for Testers and agile Teams, Addison-Wesley-Longman, Amsterdam, 2009

[2] Cunningham, W.: "The Wgcash Portfolio Management System" Proc. of ACM Object-Oriented Programming Systems, Languages and Applications – DOPSLA, New Orleans, 1992, S.29

[3] Curtis, B./ Sappidi, J./ Szynkarski, A.: "Estimating the Principle of an Application's Technical Debt", IEEE Software, Dez. 2012, S. 34

[4] Duvall, P.: Continuous Integration, Addison-Wesley, Reading Mass., 2012

[5] Kruchten, P./Nord, R.: „Technical Debt – from Metaphor to Theory and Practice". IEEE Software, Dez. 2012, S. 18

[6] Lim, E./Taksande, N./Seaman, C.: "A Balancing Act – What Practioneers say about Technical Debt", IEEE Software, Dez. 2012, S. 22

[7] Sterling, C.: Managing Software Debt – Building for inevitable Change, Addison-Wesley, 2011

MODEL-BASED SECURITY TESTING BASED ON ATTACK PATTERNS

Josip Bozic, Franz Wotawa[4]
Institute for Software Technology
Graz University of Technology
A-8010 Graz, Austria
{jbozic,wotawa}@ist.tugraz.at

Model-based testing approaches, which include white-box and black-box techniques, concentrate on testing the application whether it behaves according to a model of the SUT. Respectively, the tester may have complete insight in the program's internal structure or he does not know anything at all. For this case, several methods have been proposed, which may use randomized approaches like fuzzing or smarter methods that include evolutionary algorithms, model inference, mutation testing etc. An overview of some of the state-of-the-art techniques as well as some additional ideas can be found in [0].

The same authors introduce a different approach in [0] by relying on automatic test case creation and execution by modeling attack patterns in form of a UML state machine instead of modeling or trying to find out the internal structure of the SUT. The authors labeled this method as attack-pattern based testing. In this approach, first the attack pattern of a specific software exploitation attack has been specified. In their examples, the authors modeled both types of cross-site scripting (XSS) attacks and tried out SQL injection (SQLI) as well and used their approach in order to test web applications. After the model is set up, the execution takes place, which will submit malicious inputs against the SUT and return feedback about the result of the execution. If the test case was negative, another input is being generated and the model returns to a previously active state, executing the next input against the application again. This process continues as long as no positive feedback is encountered or no more test cases can be generated. The goal of this approach is to generate such malicious input, so that the SUT is tested at least against known vulnerabilities so that the developer can guarantee the resistance against up-to-date vulnerabilities. Further, the model allows inputting new data even after the model is already defined so the model is easily extendable.

The idea is to integrate the attack-pattern based testing technique into the software development process. Also, it may be used in regression testing.

In order to model an attack pattern, the open-source tool-kit YAKINDU Statechart Tools[5] is used, which offers an integrated modeling environment in order to model and execute event-driven systems in form of UML statecharts. Additionally, a HttpClient[6] has been specified, which is able to communicate with a web application by relying on HTTP. The responses from the SUT are parsed with the help of a DOM parser, which extracts HTML elements, e.g. scripts, images etc.
The advantage of this approach is that the browser is not used for communication with the application so all browser-intern input filters are completely evaded.

---

[4] Authors are listed in alphabetical order.
[5] http://statecharts.org/
[6] http://hc.apache.org/httpcomponents-client-ga/

After the attack pattern is specified, the tester models the state machine manually. He also has to have in mind all possible variables, which must be defined in order for the execution to begin. This approach was tested on simple PHP applications, which were deployed on the Apache server and had a common MySQL database. Afterwards, the same approach was tested against some more sophisticated web applications with additional security levels of input filters.

Figures 1 and 2 depict simple models for demonstration purposes.

First, two interfaces are specified, respectively one for the attacker and one for the system under test. All variables are attached to one of these two interfaces. A method has to be declared as an operation although the actual method is implemented in a Java class outside the model and may be called externally from the model at every time during execution.

The execution of the model begins in the initial state. The guard of the first transition requires from the tester to submit the URL address of the SUT and once this precondition is satisfied, the action is triggered and the execution succeeds in entering the next state. After entering the state, its entry action is executed and when leaving it, an exit action is carried out. In both cases, the variable values are set dynamically as can be seen in the simulation view.

Then, a method is called by submitting the input string. This method will use this address to make an authentication and if the result is ok, the next state is entered, followed by the final state where the execution terminates. Otherwise, the choice in the model continues following the alternate transition, leading to a formerly active state.

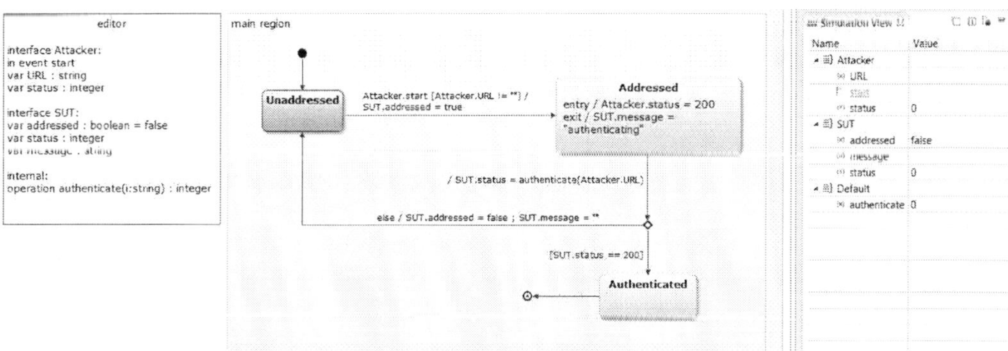

Figure 1: Initial state of the model.

This is just a small example of the testing system but as can be seen, some application specific user input is still required although the overall attack pattern model is kept as abstract as possible, so it may be applied for different web applications.

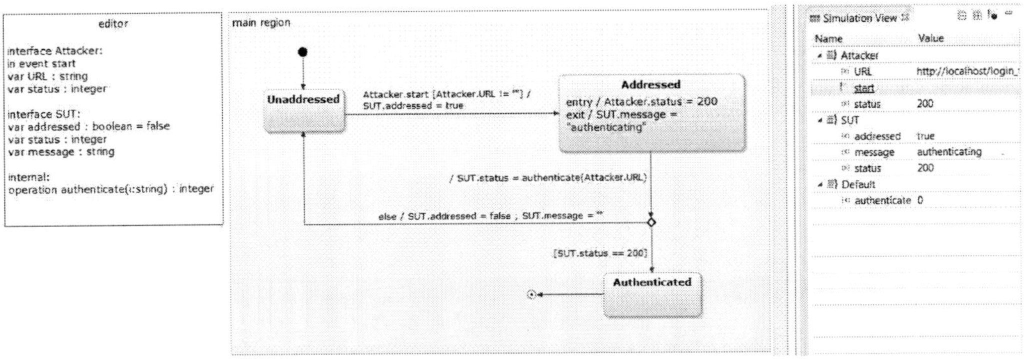

Figure 2: Final state of the model.

In order to detect SQLI or XSS vulnerability, either an expected value has to be specified or -in case of XSS- the parser encounters a *<script>* element when parsing the HTTP response from the SUT after previously submitting a malicious input. XSS leaks are somehow more difficult to trigger because the application may use some script elements by default. In that case, the tester has to specify the encounter of additional script elements (images, iframes etc.) as an indicator for vulnerability. Also in order to detect stored XSS, the combination with SQLI can be used, first by saving a script into the database and then by reading the entries with a SQL command.

Regarding the test case generation, an unsuccessful input is submitted to a test case generation method, which performs some tester specified operation, e.g. mutates the string by omitting free spaces, URL encoding, double encoding, using higher cases etc. Then, the new string is returned to the model and the execution continues by submitting the new input against the SUT again. As can be seen, it remains the task of the tester to specify the method of test case generation.

The advantage of this approach is the openness for the tester to add new features to the model, e.g. to define how a vulnerability is detected or new mutation methods. It was also tested on some already known web applications like Damn Vulnerable Web Application (DVWA)[7], NOWASP (Mutillidae)[8] and BodgeIt[9] with positive results.

The same attack pattern approach may be applied for other attack types and HttpClient also enables some additional features like the handling of cookies, which may also play a role in exploiting web applications.

REFERENCES

[1] J. Bozic and F. Wotawa, "Model-based Testing - From Safety to Security," in Proceedings of the 9th Workshop on Systems Testing and Validation (STV'12), October 2012, pp. 9–16.

[2] J. Bozic and F. Wotawa, "XSS Pattern for Attack Modeling in Testing," in Proceedings of the 2013 Eighth International Workshop on Automation of Software Test (AST'13), 2013.

[7]http://www.dvwa.co.uk/

[8]http://sourceforge.net/projects/mutillidae/

[9]https://code.google.com/p/bodgeit/

AN APPROACH TO PENETRATION TESTING VIA COMBINATORIAL DESIGNS

Dimitris E. Simos[10a] and Severin Winkler[b]

[a]SBA Research

Vienna, 1040, Austria

dsimos@sba-research.org

[b]Security Research

Vienna, 1040, Austria

swinkler@securityresearch.at

Software testing is an important but expensive part of the software development process. In this work, we are concerned with the problem of designing test plans for software systems. With the term test plan we mean a procedure that allows a systematic approach to be carried out for testing a software system. For example, suppose we want to test a software system that has 20 parameters, with 10 possible values each. Significant challenges arise in this scenario. As usual, exhaustive search (testing) is out of the question: 10^{20} tests would require billions of years to execute. Clearly, exhaustive search of search space increases time needed exponentially. We could test all 10 values for each parameter with only 10 tests, but that is unlikely to be sufficient.

To design a test plan, the tester identifies possible output values from each of the stages of the software system. It is important to find a test plan that is not too large, but yet tests for most of the interactions among the possible outputs in the modules of a software system. Recently, some researchers [1] suggested that some faults or errors in software systems are a combination of a few parameters when compared to the total parameters of the system under investigation. This observation sparked a whole new approach to automate software testing procedures through the use of combinatorial mathematics which led to the notion of combinatorial testing. There are different methodologies for combinatorial testing, and in this work we focus on the use of combinatorial designs, i.e. arrays that will be used to generate a set of test plans. Combinatorial testing is motivated by the selection of a few tests in such a manner that good coverage is still achievable. The combinatorial test design process can be briefly described as follows:

1) Model the input space. The model is expressed in terms of stages (parameters) and stage (parameter) values.
2) The model is input into a combinatorial design procedure to generate a combinatorial object that is simply an
   array of symbols.
3) Every column of the generated array is used to output a test plan of the software system.

One of the benefits of this approach, is that steps 2. and 3. can be completely automated. For more details, on combinatorial test design procedures for software testing we refer to [2].

We followed this approach to model penetration testing procedures in terms of combinatorial testing methodologies.

---

10 Authors are listed in alphabetical order.

According to CISSP certification guide, penetration testing can be roughly defined as the process of simulating attacks on a network and its systems, at the request of the owner or senior management. In particular, experimental results we have undertaken so far suggest that two to three-way combinations of the parameters involved into a software suite tested for security vulnerabilities are sufficient to reach almost 100 percent coverage in some cases.

These experimental results make penetration testing procedures an ideal candidate for modelling via combinatorial designs. Some of the problems, we aim to solve with this approach are to generate test plans and characterize vulnerabilities. It would be enlightening also if this approach can also provide a framework for automated detection of such vulnerabilities. For our approach we use the notion of mixed-level covering arrays (a specific class of combinatorial designs).
A mixed-level covering array denoted by $M\ CA(t, k, (g_1, \ldots, g_k))$ is an $k \times N$ array in which the entries of the i-th row arise from an alphabet of size g_i. Let $\{i_1, \ldots, i_t\} \subseteq \{1, \ldots, k\}$ and consider the subarray of size $t \times N$ by selecting rows of the MCA. There are $g_{1} \times \ldots \times g_t$ possible t-tuples that could appear as columns, and an MCA requires that each appears at least once (c.f. [3]). The parameter t is also called the strength of the MCA.
We exemplify this definition with the following toy example which also serves as a cornerstone of our approach.

Example: The goal is to design test plans for penetration testing. The stages of the software system are:

1) User Input can be capital or small letters and quotes
2) Validation for SQL injection with values yes and no
3) User database interaction with values true and false
4) Validation for cross-site scripting (XSS) with values yes and no

A trivial analysis indicates that we have three binary stages and one with three stage values, therefore a total of $3 \times 2^3 = 24$ different scenarios. Our goal is to reduce the number of test scenarios while still be able to test all two-way interactions (i.e. user input, validation for SQL injection). The rows of the covering array correspond to the different stages. The length of the alphabet used for he encoding of each row depends on the number of stages values. Finally, coverage property is nsured from the strength of the array. We provide bellow the desired test scenarios that are generated from MCA(2, 4, (2, 2, 2, 3)):

User Input	0	1	2	0	1	2
SQL Injection	0	1	0	1	0	1
User DB Interaction	0	0	1	1	1	0
XSS	0	1	1	1	0	0

- Selecting any two columns with binary encoding each the following 2-tuples must appear at east once: 00, 01, 11.
- Selecting any two columns with binary and ternary encoding, respectively, the following 2-tuples must appear at least once: 00, 01, 02, 11, 12.

If we decode the values of the MCA in the stage parameter values we get the following test configurations:

User Input	caps	small	quotes	caps	small	quotes
SQL Injection	no	yes	no	yes	no	yes
User DB Inter.	false	false	true	true	true	false
XSS	no	yes	yes	yes	no	no

Each column of the test configuration gives a test plan that can be used by a penetration tester to test the software system for possible vulnerabilities. It is worthwhile to note that by respecting two-way interactions, we achieve a 65 percent reduction on total number of test plans.

As future research, we plan to automate test plans for penetration testing procedures by taking into account more parameters (besides SQL injection and XSS) and implement a test suite incorporating our combinatorial design approach.

Acknowledgements

This research has received funding from the Austrian Research Promotion Agency (FFG) under grant 832185 (MOdel-Based SEcurity Testing In Practice) and the Austrian COMET Program (FFG). The work of the first author was carried out during the tenure of an ERCIM "Alain Bensoussan" Fellowship Programme. The research leading to these results has received funding from the European Union Seventh Framework Programme (FP7/2007-2013) under grant agreement no. 246016.

REFERENCES

[1] R. Kuhn, Y. Lei, and R. Kacker, "Practical combinatorial testing: Beyond pairwise," IT Professional, vol. 10, no. 3, pp. 19–23, 2008.

[2] A. P. Mathur, Foundations of Software Testing. Pearson Education, 2008.

[3] C. J. Colbourn and J. H. Dinitz, Handbook of Combinatorial Designs, Second Edition (Discrete Mathematics and Its Applications). Chapman & Hall/CRC, 2006.

Crowdsourced Software Testing: A New Approach to Quality

Georg Hansbauer
Testbirds GmbH
Radlkoferstraße 2, 81373 München
g.hansbauer@testbirds.de

Software development and testing has become increasingly challenging in recent years. Different platforms, mobile devices and agile development add to the complexity of the process, while the time-to-market is reduced. To achieve high-quality software, traditional testing methods reach their limits when it comes to the diversity of devices, operating systems and screen resolutions. In addition, user expectations have never been so high and the tolerance for issues never been so low. As a result, these changes require new ways of testing: A new method called crowdtesting addresses many of the challenges development teams face today.

1. Software Testing in the Real World

Crowdtesting combines testing with the principle of crowdsourcing. Crowdtesting is a form of outsource testing, which is undertaken by a mass of internet users (the crowd). The crowd is working on a defined problem and supports the company with its proposed solutions. Crowdtesting uses this concept to test websites, mobile apps, games, or enterprise software in order to get rid of bugs and to optimize the user experience. This way, software can be tested under real conditions on a variety of devices by a desired target group - even before the release. The range of possibilities varies from a full service functional and usability test to self-service concepts, where the provider only connects the client to the crowd through an online platform. Either way, maintaining high quality results is crucial. Since the testers are working remotely, the setup and documentation need to be monitored closely for the development team to make use of the results. This is achieved by either the crowdtesting provider or the client himself.

2. The Process

The first step of each crowd-based test is a briefing that defines the conditions of the test. What kind of setup is needed and how can this be realized in the test? This includes, among other things, the focus of the project (Bug-finding, usability testing or combined testing), the target group of the software and the devices, as well as operating systems that should be part of the test. The setup so far is similar to a traditional testing project. Now, however, it has to be translated into a test description for the users in the crowd. The project manager sets up the project on the online platform and makes the software available for the carefully selected testers depending on their devices and demographic data. For web-based tests, access to the software is achieved through some kind of access data, for example to a staging system. Mobile applications can be distributed through a dedicated app store on the crowdtesting provider's platform before release, whether it is Android or iOS. The users are then able to test in their familiar surroundings, using their own devices, and are therefore able to provide unbiased information compared to the developers or in-house testers. Each tester documents his or her work in the form of process descriptions and screenshots or screencasts.

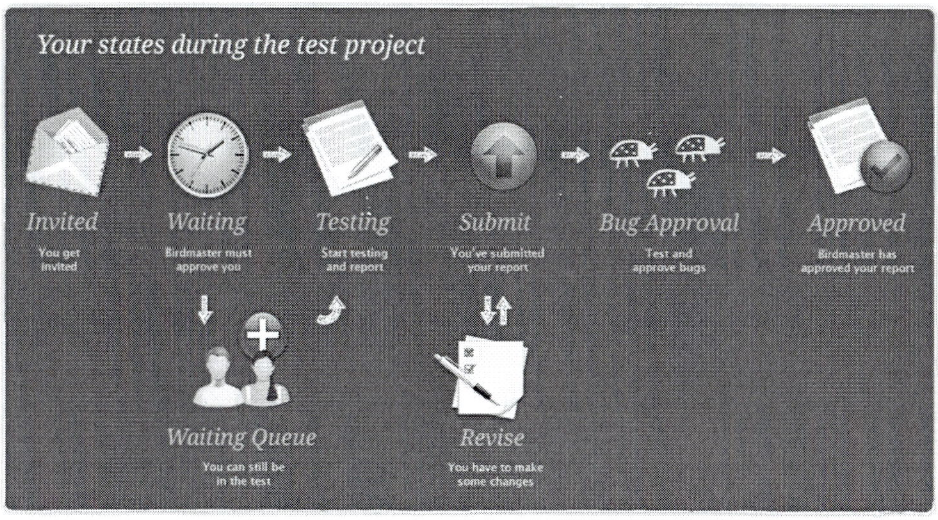

Figure 1: Crowdtesting workflow for testers.

3. Benefits and Challenges

The crowd consists of real users who test software flexibly, which means they are available on demand. Consumers can also reflect reality better than traditional in-house testing methods. In addition, the crowd has various combinations of devices, operating systems and browsers already at hand, which would be almost impossible simulate or to supply for an internal lab. This large pool of thousands of different testers allows the selection of specific target groups, as well as recreational testers or even certified testers. Since the testing process is fast and flexible in itself, it can be integrated into existing release cycles and identified shortcomings can be corrected immediately. Crowdtesting allows testing in different stages of the development ranging from the evaluation of prototypes to a final check at the end of the beta-phase. Both aspects, the availability of real users and devices, allow for a significant improvement of the software in order to address issues and fix problems before it becomes too expensive.

The issue of maintaining quality is crucial for crowdtesting. Since everybody can sign up to become a crowd-tester, new testers have to pass a qualifications test in order to participate in paid projects. This test is similar to a normal project and serves as a means for testers to get to know the platform and its requirements. In each test, a project manager reviews all reports and bugs submitted by the testers for completeness, traceability and quality. Only then will they be accepted and cleared for customers to see on their backend. Otherwise, the tester has to revise the submitted content until the desired quality is reached. Test protocols also include screenshots or even screencasts in order to ensure test coverage. If the crowd is accessed through a self-service model, it is crucial that the client has a dedicated project manager himself. He is responsible for the test cycle and ideally has some experience with remote test management, since the quality of the results depend on the management of the participants.

4. An Addition to Internal Testing

In summary, there are several requirements for crowdtesting to be successful:

1. The setup has to fit a remote test
2. The right testers need to be selected (target group and/or experts)
3. Documentation is crucial to ensure test coverage

If these conditions are met, crowdtesting can supplement traditional software testing methods and offer valuable insights on how the software performs in the real world. Since the crowd is not involved in the development of the application itself, unbiased feedback is one of the benefits. In short, user acceptance is a critical factor. Due to the diverse coverage of various device combinations, bugs can be identified on almost all devices. In a traditional environment, this testing would be immensely time-consuming and expensive.

It is important to note that in-house testing is still vitally important for the success of the software. However, an ever-growing spectrum of devices combined with rising user expectations make for a tight race among competitors in any market. As a result, it can be the little things deciding over the success or failure of an application. Under the right conditions, crowdtesting can secure a competitive advantage and become a continuous part of the testing process.

PRACTICAL GUIDELINES FOR SYSTEM TESTING WITH DEFECT TAXONOMIES

Michael Felderer[1], Armin Beer[2]
[1] University of Innsbruck, Innsbruck, Austria
michael.felderer@uibk.ac.at
[2] Beer Test Consulting, Baden, Austria
info@arminbeer.at

Abstract
Defect taxonomies can be seamlessly integrated into a standard test process and improve the effectiveness of system testing. In this paper we presents practical guidelines for system testing with defect taxonomies learned from industrial application of the approach.

1. Overview of System Testing with Defect Taxonomies

In practice, most defect taxonomies are only used for the a-posteriori allocation of testing resources to prioritize failures for debugging purposes. But the full potential of these taxonomies to control and improve all phases of the overall system test process has so far remained unexploited. To overcome this limitation, in previous publications [1,2,3] we defined and evaluated system testing with defect taxonomies which support all phases of testing requirements, i.e. test planning, design, execution and evaluation.

Figure 1 summarizes the artifacts and application steps of system testing with defect taxonomies (STDT). On the basis of the requirements specification the defect taxonomy is created (step 1). Then the requirements are linked to defect categories and validated (step 2). Afterwards tests are planned (step 3) which results in a test strategy. From the test strategy abstract and physical test cases are designed (step 4) and then executed (step 5). Finally, the test results are evaluated and failures are assigned to defect categories (step 6). In [2] all process steps and artifacts are discussed in detail.

As mentioned before STDT supports all phases of the system test process. In the test planning phase the assignment of requirements to defect categories supports a more detailed estimation of the test effort which is additionally based on requirements artifacts, the priority of the requirements, the severity of the defect categories and the selected test design technique. In the test design phase test cases are derived based on the defect taxonomy based test strategy fixed before, i.e. the linkage between weighted defect categories, prioritized requirements, and test design techniques is exploited to derive requirements tests from requirements artifacts. The defect taxonomy based test strategy allows the design of more effective tests, i.e. tests which find more failures on average, and reduces the total number of test [2]. As the number of test cases is reduced, the overall test execution time decreases. Additionally, the test cases can be prioritized based on the requirements priority and the severity of the defect category if test execution resources are limited. Experience gained during the execution of tests and the evaluation of failures detected by these tests, are used to adapt the defect taxonomy and to optimize the number of test cases of the next releases and for regression testing purposes. As the failures are traceable to defect categories the severity values of failures which are assigned by testers and have varying accuracy, can be checked and adapted in the test evaluation phase via the severity value of its assigned defect category. This enables more precise statements about the quality of a release and decisions whether additional hotfixes or iterations are needed.

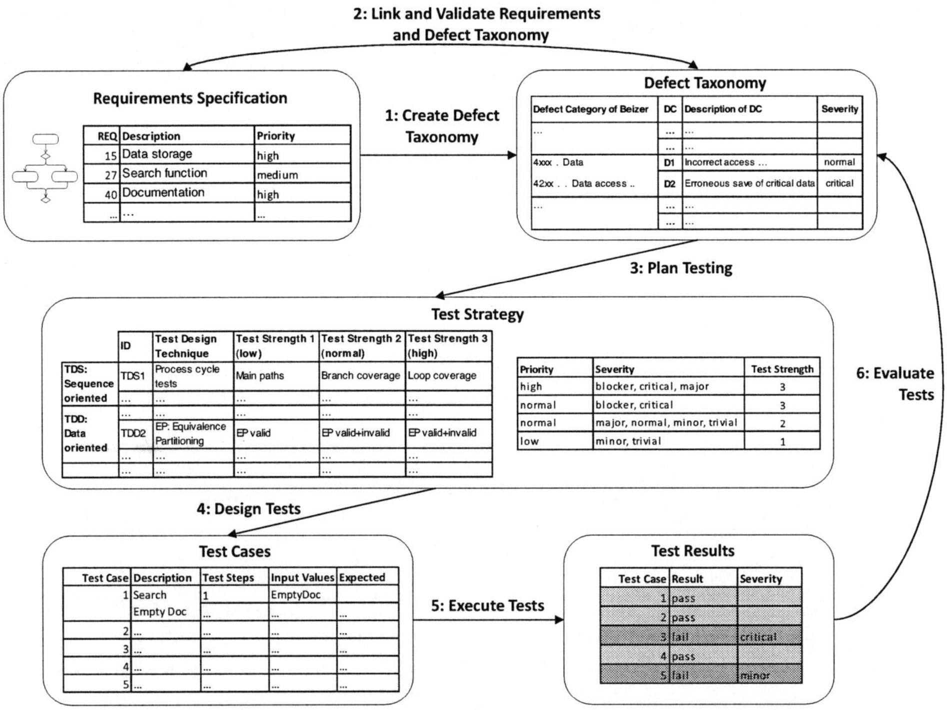

Figure 1. Steps and Artifacts of System Testing with Defect Taxonomies (STDT)

2. Practical Guidelines

In this section, we present practical guidelines for the application of STDT with respect to the management of the underlying defect taxonomy, the required tool support, the quality of requirements, preconditions of the development and test process as well as the cost-benefit analysis of the approach. The guidelines have been derived from the industrial application of STDT.

2.1 Management of Defect Taxonomies

Defect taxonomies are the central artifact of STDT and their suitability influences the quality of the results. By creating and using several defect taxonomies we learned that 4 to 9 sub-categories on each level are manageable and that each sub-category requires a clear meaning which is supported by additional exemplary defects for each sub-category. New defect taxonomies should be created on the basis of available defect data of completed projects and the feedback of affected roles such as developers or testers should be considered.

2.2 Tool Support

The additional tool support required to implement STDT is quite low as all activities specific to STDT can be done with spreadsheets. We create a defect taxonomy as well as its links to requirements (requirements were exported from the requirements management tool into a separate worksheet), test design techniques (stored in a separate worksheet) and failures (failures were exported from the defect management tool into a separate worksheet) with spreadsheets. This works well in our projects as spreadsheets are easy to customize, frequently used and manageable for analyst, domain expert as well as test manager without additional training.

2.3 Quality of Requirements

With defect taxonomies especially the requirements quality attributes completeness, ranked for importance, verifiability, traceability, comprehensibility and right level of detail can be reviewed for individual requirements, requirements artifacts or complete requirements specifications. In the projects were STDT was applied, we found several additional anomalies compared to the standard review process based on IEEE 1028 and took appropriate countermeasures to increase the quality of requirements and consequently also in the released product.

2.4. Preconditions of the Development and Test Process

STDT demands a requirements specification containing requirements with priority values and assigned requirements artifacts such as use cases and business rules to design concrete test cases. These preconditions are met by most requirements development approaches in use and shows the versatility of our approach. STDT is an extension of systematic requirements-based testing. The implementation of STDT therefore requires an established standard process for system testing, for instance based on the standard test process of the ISTQB, with clearly defined test planning, design, execution and evaluation steps. The full potential of STDT can be exploited in iterative and incremental development processes as the cost advantage of STDT compared to RT grows with the number of iterations and decisions on whether additional hotfixes are needed or when and what to release are supported by more precise information.

2.5. Cost-Benefit Analysis

As soon as requirements-based testing with defect taxonomies has been introduced in an organization by providing a description of the procedure, respective templates, and training for the testers, the effort for applying the method in a concrete project is due to our experience manageable. The main benefits of using STDT are (1) the increased quality of the requirements, tests and especially the released product as well as (2) the increased process quality providing decision support for the release and test process. The main costs of the approach are (1) the effort to create and maintain the defect taxonomy as well as (2) their linkage to requirements and failures. In addition, we defined a feasible and realistic decision procedure whether to apply STDT. The decision procedure compares the cumulated estimated time effort for STDT and system testing (ST) along the phases of STDT. We conducted this procedure in a project [1] and found that the break-even of STDT was reached already after the first iteration. With a growing number of iterations the cost difference to ST and thus also the benefit of STDT increases further.

Acknowledgements. Parts of the work described in this article were supported by the project QE LaB – Living Models for Open Systems (FFG 822740).

REFERENCES

[1] Felderer, M., Beer, A., Estimating the Return on Investment of Defect Taxonomy Supported System Testing in Industrial Projects, 38th Euromicro Conf. on Softw. Engineering and Advanced Applications (SEAA 2012), IEEE 2012.

[2] Felderer, M., Beer, A., Using Defect Taxonomies to Improve the Maturity of the System Test Process: Results from an Industrial Case Study, Software Quality Days 2013, LNBIP, Springer 2013.

[3] Felderer, M., Beer, A., Using Defect Taxonomies for Requirements Validation in Industrial Projects, 21st International Requirements Engineering Conference (RE'13), IEEE 2013.

EFFICIENT TEST-CASE GENERATION FOR COMPOSITIONAL REAL-TIME SPECIFICATIONS

Willibald Krenn, Dejan Ničković, and Loredana Tec[11]
AIT Austrian Institute of Technology GmbH
Donau-City-Straße 1
1220 Vienna, Austria
{willibald.krenn, dejan.nickovic, loredana.tec}@ait.ac.at

Abstract *We present an efficient new algorithm for mutation-based test-case generation for real-time systems, modeled as interacting networks of timed automata. Timed automata are finite state machines extended with continuous clock variables which measure time between events. The algorithm, implemented in our MoMuT::TA test case generation tool, exploits the structure of the given model to shorten the time needed for test-case generation. We give a summary of the algorithm, published in [2], and present the gains obtained by MoMuT::TA on an ex- ample model. The results suggest that this approach enables test case generation from larger models which could not be handled in the past.*

1. Introduction

Model-based mutation testing is a specific type of model-based testing in which faults are deliberately injected into the specification model. The aim of mutation-based testing techniques is to generate test cases that can detect the injected errors. This means that a generated test case shall fail if it is executed on a (deterministic) system-under-test that implements the faulty model. Like other model-based testing techniques, it suffers from the state-space explosion problem: it is difficult to explore the state-space of a complex model while achieving a specific coverage. To address this problem we developed in [2] an efficient incremental extension to the test case generation algorithm for real-time systems [1].

In [1], the model is given as a flat timed automaton with inputs and outputs (TAIO). However, if the model S is compositional, i.e. it consists of a network of $S_1 \parallel S_2 \parallel \ldots \parallel S_n$ TAIO components, the above TCG procedure may be highly inefficient. A mutant M of S has by definition a single altered feature; hence M is of the form $M_1 \parallel S_2 \parallel \ldots \parallel S_n$. While it is possible to flatten S and M by explicitly computing the parallel composition of the components and then directly apply the framework of [1], the parallel composition is likely to be very expensive and the fact that only a single component in S is mutated is not used at all. Hence, we replace the TCG algorithm from [1] with its incremental variant illustrated in Figure 1.

2. Algorithm and Evaluation

The incremental TCG algorithm (Incremental) decomposes the problem by first checking the (simpler) language inclusion of M_1 in S_1. If this check is successful, the mutant is equivalent to the

[11] The research leading to these results has received funding from ARTEMIS Joint Undertaking under grants agreement numbers 269335 (MBAT), 269265 (pSafeCer) and 295373 (nSafeCer), and from national fundings (Federal Ministry for Transport, Innovation and Technology and Austrian Research Promotion Agency) under program line "Trust in IT Systems", project number 829583 (TRUFAL).

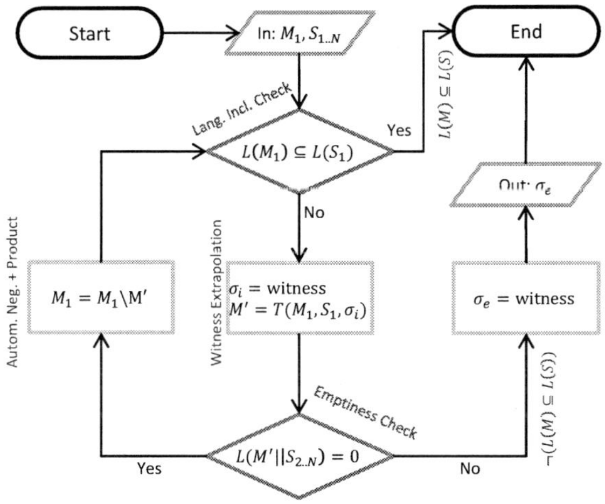

Figure 1 Incremental TCG Algorithm

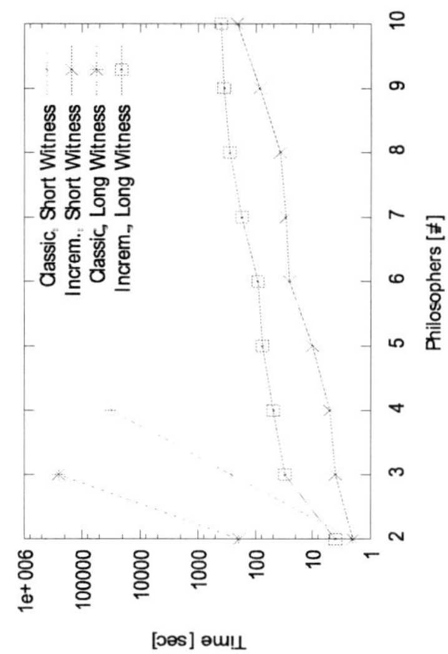

Figure 2 Run times for Incremental and Classic

original model and the algorithm terminates. Otherwise, we get a trace σ_1 witnessing the language inclusion violation between the two components. However, this witness is local to M_1 and S_1 and may be disabled in the composition, hence it may not witness the language inclusion violation of M in S. In the next step, $\sigma 1$ is extrapolated to its symbolic version M´ which encodes a set of such local witnesses. Then, we check if there is a local witness encoded in M´ that is not disabled in the composition with other components. This is done by composing iteratively M´ with S_2, ..., S_n and checking for language emptiness. If a trace σ_e showing non-emptiness of the composition is found, the same trace also witnesses that the language of M is not included in S. We then use σ_e to build a test case. Otherwise, the algorithm backtracks, removes local witnesses encoded by M´ from M1 and repeats the procedure.

Using Incremental on a Dining Philosophers model we were able to generate test cases without backtracking and achieve a speedup of over 8000x (cf. Figure 2, from 72h to 31s) compared to the classic algorithm. Our experiments also showed that Incremental is sensitive to the number of backtrackings but this constraint fits well with our application domain. Hence, we can conclude that Incremental is a game-changer: it allows MoMuT::TA to efficiently generate test cases from models that we could not handle before.

REFERENCES

[1] Bernhard K. Aichernig, Florian Lorber, and Dejan Ničković. Time for mutants - mutation testing with timed automata. In TAP, 2013.

[2] Willibald Krenn, Dejan Ničković, and Loredana Tec. Incremental language inclusion checking for networks of timed automata. In FORMATS, 2013.

VALUE-DRIVEN TESTING – THE INNER VALUE OF TEST CASES

Ingo Philipp[1], Wolfgang Platz[1], Rudolf Ramler[2]

[1] TRICENTIS Technology & Consulting GmbH
Leonard-Bernstein-Straße 10, A-1220 Vienna, Austria
{i.philipp, w.platz}@tricentis.com

[2] Software Competence Center Hagenberg GmbH
Softwarepark 21, A-4232 Hagenberg, Austria
rudolf.ramler@scch.at

Abstract
A value-driven testing approach maximizes the return on investments from software testing. This paper summarizes our work on determining the inner value of test cases for value-based requirements coverage. The paper describes how to compute the inner value of test cases and explains how this measure can be used for prioritizing test cases in value-driven testing. The implementation as part of the TOSCA Testsuite™ makes the testing approach available for software development projects in business and industry.

1. Introduction

Testing is a costly activity that operates under tight time and resource limits, especially in fast-paced software development projects in business and industry. The benefit in return of testing is risk reduction. With every executed test case, the risk of a defect in an implemented requirement is reduced. A value-driven testing approach [7] seeks to maximize the return on investment in testing and, therefore, prioritizes the test cases according to their potential contribution to reducing risks.

The prerequisite to value-driven testing is the ability to determine the potential contribution of individual test cases in order to be able to align the testing effort with the achievable benefit of testing. In this paper we show how to quantify this contribution in terms of the inner value of test cases. The described approach is an integral part of the TOSCA Testsuite™ (www.tricentis.com), making it applicable for testing large real-world systems.

The paper summarizes our previous work on value-based coverage measurement for requirements-based testing [4, 5]. The described approach extends conventional requirements-based testing by taking the implications of combinatorial test design into account [3]. These two techniques together reflect the *external perspective* and the *internal perspective* relevant for value-driven testing: First, the requirements-based priority is derived from the business value of the associated requirements and, second, the impact of the corresponding usage scenarios is derived from weighted input data combinations.

2. Background and Related Work

Most available methods and tools calculate measures for test coverage at the level of the program code. However, such a code-based coverage is a technical measure, which is only partially useful from the perspective of value-driven testing. From a value-based viewpoint, the amount of code part of the implementation of a function does not necessarily and sufficiently reflect its business value. Thus, these technical coverage measures are limited in terms of making sound statements on the value achievable from testing.

Similarly, most of the available methods, techniques and tools for software testing are value-neutral and do not realize the potential value contribution of testing [1]. As a result, test managers tend to create a large number of test cases they execute as their proof of work. The progress in testing is then simply reported in terms of the number of available test cases, the number of test executions and the number of passed or failed test runs. These value-neutral numbers do neither provide sufficient information about the extent to which the software system's functionality has actually been covered by tests nor about the extent to which the remaining quality risks jeopardize the expected value of the software product [2].

From a value-based viewpoint [1, 2, 7], test case counts have to be related to the functionality and the value of the software system under test. In order to take the results that have been achieved rather than using the effort that has been taken as a test manager's justification, an approach for value-based coverage measurement, linking the requirements-based priority (external perspective) and the usage-based impact (internal perspective), has been presented in our previous work. The approach is based on [3, 4, 5] to its full extent and outlined below.

3. Approach

The external dimension is concerned with ensuring the priorities of the external stakeholder. The system under test is structured to the requirements (e.g. functional units), which are then associated with an anticipated business value. According to the general guidelines for risk assessment [6] the requirement's business value is inverted to a business risk expressing the extent of the potential loss of a required functionality. This requirements-driven risk-based approach enables to align the testing effort with the achievable benefit of testing.

The business risk associated to the requirements is inherited to the corresponding test cases, whereas a test case exercises a part of a requirement with a defined set of input data values associated to different data attributes. The input data values are combined to test cases using different combinatorial testing techniques [3]. Several input data combinations, i.e. usage scenarios, may be necessary to cover a particular requirement. However, from the business perspective of testing, these input data combinations are not equally important. The significance of different test cases in context of a requirement varies greatly since, for example, standard scenarios are more important as they occur more frequently, affect a larger number of users and have a higher impact on the business value than exotic scenarios, such as boundary cases or invalid scenarios.

The information on usage scenarios is included by determining the *inner value* of test cases from their business relevant degrees of freedom, i.e. input data values and data attributes. Thereby, the *inner value* of a test case is defined by assigning weights to its business relevant degrees of freedom. Then these weights are normed appropriately and finally aggregated to the overall contribution of a test case to the test coverage. The contribution of individual test cases, i.e. their business-based test coverage, can only be determined exactly prior to test execution if and only if the calculation logic of the business-based test coverage is independent from the test result and the order of test execution, when the input data values are used across several tests. In order to guarantee this all, a new combinatorial testing technique, known as *Linear Expansion* (www.tricentis.com), has been introduced.

5. Conclusions

As shown in [3], *Linear Expansion* satisfies the requirements, constraints and practical needs of large real-world projects, where testing is a central quality assurance that consumes a considerable share of the overall effort, and outperforms other combinatorial coverage criteria such as the all combinations coverage, each choice coverage and pair-wise coverage.

The proposed approach goes beyond conventional requirements-based testing where the value of tests is primarily determined on the basis of the requirement's estimated business values or risks. It therefore extends the conventional best practice of requirements-based testing. The approach described above, known as *LinearQ*, has been implemented as part of the TOSCA Testsuite™ and was successfully applied in real-world projects. As shown in [4] this value-based approach clearly outperforms a value-neutral approach and it also supersedes the conventional requirements-based approach. The results obtained demonstrate that this method supports for relating testing to the underlying business value. The application of this approach to real-world projects shows that the higher the targeted test performance is the higher the potential savings will be.

REFERENCES

[1] Boehm, B., Value-Based Software Engineering, ACM SIGSOFT Software Engineering Notes, vol. 28, p. 12, March 2003.

[2] Li, Q., F. Shu, B. Boehm and Q. Wang, Improving the ROI of software quality assurance activities: an empirical study. In Proceedings of the 2010 international conference on new modeling concepts for today's software processes, pp. 357-368, 2010.

[3] Ramler, R., T. Kopetzky and W. Platz, Combinatorial test design in the TOSCA Testsuite: Lessons learned and practical implications. In Proceedings of the 5th International Conferences on Software Testing, Verification and Validation, pp. 569-572, IEEE, 2012.

[4] Ramler, R., T. Kopetzky and W. Platz, Taking a Business Perspective in Testing ERP Systems with Value-Based Requirements Coverage. In proceeding of ERP Future 2012 , Springer, 2012.

[5] Ramler, R., T. Kopetzky and W. Platz, Value-Based Coverage Measurement in Requirements-Based Testing: Lessons Learned from an Approach Implemented in the TOSCA Testsuite. In Proceedings of the 38th Euromicro Conference on Software Engineering and Advanced Applications, pp. 363-366, IEEE, 2012.

[6] Pandian, C., Applied Software Risk Management: A Guide for Software Project Managers. Auerbach Publications, 2006.

[7] Sneed, H., Value Driven Testing. In Proceedings of the 2009 Testing: Academic and Industrial Conference - Practice and Research Techniques pp. 157-166, IEEE, 2009.